T0156703

THE LIGHT
THROUGH
THE WOODS

DREAMS OF SURVIVAL OF HUMAN
SOUL IN THE AGE OF TECHNOLOGY

MAHARAJ KAUL

iUniverse, Inc.
New York Bloomington

The Light through the Woods
Dreams of Survival of Human Soul in the Age of Technology

iUniverse books may be ordered through booksellers or by contacting:

iUniverse
1663 Liberty Drive
Bloomington, IN 47403
www.iuniverse.com
1-800-Authors (1-800-288-4677)

Because of the dynamic nature of the Internet, any Web addresses or links contained in this book may have changed since publication and may no longer be valid. The views expressed in this work are solely those of the author and do not necessarily reflect the views of the publisher, and the publisher hereby disclaims any responsibility for them.

ISBN: 978-1-4502-3354-5 (sc)
ISBN: 978-1-4502-3355-2 (dj)
ISBN: 978-1-4502-3356-9 (ebook)

Library of Congress Control Number: 2010907573

Printed in the United States of America

iUniverse rev. date: 06/10/2010

The love, the care, and the support of the people indicated below has helped me to cross the many valleys of anguish, which life inexorably puts human beings through.

This book is dedicated to:

My sister, Lalita, who has all her life given love and care to her family and friends. In life gray or shining, she has burnt her flame bright.

My brother, Babu, who possesses mettle meeting challenges of life, keenness of mind, and love for his family.

My brother, Kaka, who with his elegant aloofness, tenacious persistence, and charming modesty has carved a unique place in the family. He walks with his feet more firmly on ground than anyone else in the family.

My wife, Mohini, whose lake of love has never lowered its level and whose generosity has always been ample.

Other Books By Maharaj Kaul

Meditation On Time

Destruction And Injustice:
The Tribulations Of Kashmiri Pandits

Life With Father

Inclinations And Reality:
The Search For The Absolute

CONTENTS

MANY MIRRORED MOSAIC

1. The Light Through The Woods 3

2. Looking At The Lake 6

3. The City And The Village 9

4. Many Splendorous Faces Of Eternity 14

5. Driving On I-84 18

6. On The Way To Eternity..21

7. A Reflection From The Mirror Of God 24

8. The Meaning Of Love...26

9. It Rained In Rockland Yesterday 27

10. In A Woman's Bosom 29

11. But Alas The World Has Tied My Hands...........31

12. A Cup Of Tea 33

13. Seeing Through A Window 35

14. Sometimes I Think The Poetry Of Human Heart
    Will Never Die 37

15. Elysium Of Loneliness 39

16. Flowers.. 42

17. Dreams..43

18. Peace...45

BEAUTIFUL PAIN

19. Perspective Of Time...49

20. The Mercy Of Montessory Beach 52

21. She Has Changed...56

22. Who Am I ? 60

23. A Leaf Falls 62

24. Why Do I Keep My Lonely Ways? 64

25. Soul Of The Modern Man 65

26. The Nature Of Man 67

27. Is That What Is Human Life? 69

28. Walking The Last Footsteps In The World 72

29. There Is No Time 74

VIGNETTES OF TIME

30. Lana Takes Retirement 79

31. What Will You Do When I Am Gone? 82

32. Elegance At A Rain-ruined Rural Party 84

33. Do Not Open The Doors To My Childhood 85

34. Father 86

35. The Mood Of An Evening At Bellmore Island 87

36. Dali 89

37. Thinking Of Surinder 91

38. A Light Shines In Andover 93

39. A Marriage Made In Heaven 94

40. For A Life Yet On Fire 96

41. Will They Still Hold Their Hands Together? 97

42. I Met A Boy In San Francisco 99

43. Tricia 100

44. Chasing The Shadows Of Dadu 101

45. Anniversary 102

46. It Seems Only Yesterday 103

47. You Came And Lit Up The Evening 105

DREAMS OF PAST

48. Upon Waking Up On My Birthday 109

49. A Rendezvous At Habba Kadal 110

50. Nadir Munjays At Tarakh Halwoy's Shop 113

51. Irrepressible Youth 116

52. The Agony Of Dal Lake 126

53. The Anguish Of Kashmiri Pandits 131

54. The Glory And The Exile 132

55. Roots 136

MANY MIRRORED MOSAIC

The tapestry of life hung before me
As a vast inscrutable enigma,
Pieces of which were so well integrated
That the whole looked a beautiful and divine work of art.
Yet its experience in the world
Was fraught with awe, fear, and pain.
The challenge to unravel it has bedeviled me all my life,
Causing me much anguish as well as joy.

The Light Through The Woods

I have just tossed the stack of unpaid bills to the far corner of my room,
Bundled up the junk mail for the Monday garbage pickup,
While the newspapers lie strewn unopened on the dinette.
I want to leave the chains of the world behind me,
Pack up my knapsack
And journey up to see the light through the woods.

The woods are two hours on a bike,
Secluded in the rear rising plateau of the Morton Mountains,
Where slender and tall oaks mingle with wild shrubs and flowers,
The riotous brooks bubble over the moss covered rocks,
And the light dances through the enigmatic chiaroscuros,
Where the splendor of nature merges with the splendor of imagination.

Here in the kingdom of the filtered light
Trees bend with fluid grace, leaves fall with solemn dignity.
Human footsteps are an intrusion in the music of eternity,
But the rustling of leaves with wind adds to the music of silence.
Every movement is electric, every thought seems to be burgeoning for
the first time,
Every tree and every blade of grass seems unique, every hue resplendent.

Walking through the leaf and flower decked path,
In the intertwined ribbon of light and shade,
With every tree trunk a knot in the green embroidery,
Each treetop aspiring to touch the infinite blue above,
Every wildflower a greeting to the journey ahead –
The journey without a destination.

The hallowed tapestry of the woods unfolds with a silent splash.
As one walks over myriad paths through the trees – undefined but
yet leading forward,
One encounters light that is filtered bright but appears multi-sourced:
Diffused, concaved, sanguine, multi-hued, a fine multilayered sfumato,
In effulgent opulence – a latticed fabric creating a maze of prisms -
A stream of vibrant crystal concatenations.

The trees reference the sheet of epileptic torrent of light cascading
through them –
Earthly sentinels of the rushing infinite.
Each path in the woods appears leading to an unknown place,
Each falling leaf embraces you with tender and silent grace.
The tree branches slice light multi-layered and the sky blue sneaks
edging them.
Talking breaks the echo of eternity, walking disturbs the halo of infinity.

There is a heart of loneliness in the woods,
A womb forever pregnant.
Man feels melting into the scene – a natural integration.
The tapestry of the hallowed light beckons to an unknown point.
The realm ahead appears enchanting and eternal,
While the world behind seems receding into insignificance.

The light coming through the woods evokes a new imagination,
A dream of a new world, a vision of a new life.
It is a message of liberation and new meaning,
It asks for giving and not possession, being and not becoming.
Climbing up the Morton Mountains, wrapped in woods,
The heights permit a wide and a penetrating view of the world below
where man lives.

A blade of grass has more wisdom than a library full of books,
A sunset is more rewarding than a week's bull market on Wall St.
Where have we lost the mind in the matter, the spirit in the process;
Where have we lost the miracle of nature, the life in the world.
Man is trapped in the petty materialistic schemes of his brain,
While the light through the woods lies unexplored in front of him.

Looking At The Lake

I am looking at Lake George, New York, while walking its careless, distraught contour.
I see the immensity of its beauty, carried over thousands of years.
A magnificent work of God bestowed with long-lasting splendor,
To remind man of his banishment from the heavens.

A lake is God's message of how sublime He can be.
An envelope of water mirroring human life.
It has life's fullness, circumference, inner turmoil, and external storms.
It has infinite expressibility; it has points of personality but it is its wholeness which communicates with us.
A lake does not tell us what it is; to different observers it is their own projection of it.
It is a body of water with purpose, but with a demeanor of purposelessness.

Lake George is a masterstroke of imagination,
Reminding its visitors, from generation to generation,
The power and benevolence of nature over our lives.
A mirror we can hold to see ourselves in it.

I stand before the lake and
Wonder at the nature of nature,
And man's relevance in the cosmic scheme.

I have roamed around the planet earth for many decades
And am now near the last turns of my end.

My life is only a little tale in the infinite tapestry of the universe,
Which I have tried to keep in check from the human vanity and ego.

I look at the lake and feel an eternity grab me,
My life seems to be an infinite ribbon forever uncoiling.

Reflected in the lake I see the colossal cosmos aglow in inhuman splendor,
Its apparent infinitude dazzles the senses out of me,
Its mystery mesmerizes me to a permanent wonder.

In the lake I see an arrest of the cosmic splendor,
A micro-capsule of the energy and enigma of the universe.

Why is universe as it is, why was it made in the first place.
The absurdity of these questions is apparent, as universe does not
have a human mind.
It exists by its own design, it is aglow by its own light.
It has always been there and it will always be there.

For man to understand these things is a liberation from earthly shackles,
A reunion with eternity, a stepping into the cosmic dance.

Human life was not meant to be lived as it is generally,
Man carries too much worthless baggage with him –
The artless designs of his scheming brain.
Man stands as a caricature of his natural majesty,
A wasted spark in the worldly morass.

A lake is controlled mass but with infinite expressions,
It is a circumscribed possession but forever echoing liberation,
Its circumference aches to expand, its surface desires to dance off to
evaporation,
Its feet are on ground but its heart is dancing to the other drummer,
It appears static but it is a dynamic state of shifting masses.
A lake is a cosmic dance with a human face.

A lake is ripeness at ease with itself,
Grace forever held by its weight.
It aspires the dance of waves but is content to remain within its shores,
Freedom never squandered in rash adventures of an ocean or a river.

If man could only be like a lake,
Finite but soaring in its spirit,
Bounded but bursting to expand,
Possessed but with flexible circumference,
Static in composure but dynamic in disposition,
Effervescent in its longings but controlled in its demeanor.

A lake is brimming with hope that tomorrow will be better,
Because its guts have churned enough and its bosom has heaved enough,
Its patience has stretched long,
And has no theatrics to play.

A lake is a human condition,
Structured yet fluid,
Like life a lake is just a ripple across time,
Where imagination gives it context and meaning.
A lake is a slice of human heart resting on God's little fingers.

The City And The Village

Dedicated to my friend Roy Friedman, who left us before his time.
A playwright, a family man, and a friend, who had yet to offer his best.

My grandmother told me that I was born many years ago,
Somewhere in the rural world of Tulsa County, New Whitman.
My mother had died when I was one, father having left her earlier.

Tulsa is sculptured with vast, irregularly undulating green fields,
Draped with stable but mercurial, thin, open blue skies.
In the mornings I opened my eyes to unfiltered, bold, golden sunshine;
At nights I closed them moved by inky black skies, dotted
By a flux of shapeless, glowing but flickering light points called stars.

Childhood streamed with delightful ease;
Everything was connected, everything was afire.
There was no beginning and there was no end.
Playing on the seashore of time, every moment was precious –
Yet every moment was dispensable.

There was an inner time, more relevant than the outer time.
There was an inner freedom, stronger than the outer one.
Youth curved down by its own fullness,
And eternity seemed within grasp.
Every moment was possessed, but every moment was a mystery.

But one day the shimmering galleon of youth was pierced by a hidden rock.
The punctured hull started pulling the ship down.
Tulsa was running out of good paying jobs,
The specter of starvation loomed large on the skies
And the dreams of youth leaked through the hole of economy.

The lack of bread forced me to leave Tulsa
And find refuge in the gargantuan metropolis of Nolan,
Some two hundred seventy miles southwest of Tulsa.
I entered a new stage of life, where survival was more than a peace of mind—
It was a confrontation with the elements of life.

I was lucky to find a job in a small factory on the outskirts of the city,
Called Bright Lights, where I had to assemble lighting fixtures,
Which were used on the tables and ceilings of homes -
Low-end products used by financially challenged new immigrants
and students.
The work was fast-moving, coordinated, and exhilarating.

On the sixth floor of a tenement, I landed a walk-up efficiency,
Equipped with a kitchenette, bath, and closet.
It was smaller than my Tulsa place but had personality and style.
Through its window it let in Nolan's exuberance, color, and vigor.
Living in it felt like being on an island in a sea of activity and excitement.

At five in the morning, reminiscent of my rural existence,
I woke up to start the long day to my work.
From my room to the public bus, I walked three miles.
The bus took an hour before I climbed it down
For one-mile walk to my factory.

Nolan knocked me off the ground when I arrived from Tulsa.
Looking by the unfettered eyes of a villager,
The city was a gigantic enterprise of man.
Here was a world with a different foundation than I had known it:
A vision more complex than I thought was good for man.

The evening is city's time,
When the commercial jostling and greediness of the day
Transforms to sleek sophistication of glamour and whispers.
There is lightness in the feet and a twinkle in the eyes
In anticipation of what might happen.

The city packages its thrills in brilliant allure,
Ignoring man's inner conflicts, titillating his senses,
Glorifying the moment, celebrating the instincts.
It delivers its wares instantaneously,
Short-circuiting the thought process.

Every city signals silently that it is a gift box
Full of exciting candies for delectation.
The sexual candy is the biggest candy it has to offer
And it is wrapped in a thousand different ways.
More powerful than the product itself,
Is the titillation at the prospect of acquiring it.

Nolan offered a scintillating array of intellectual and cultural media:
Museums, theaters, seminars, movies, bookshops, talks, etc.
It seemed a feast for the mind, an expanse for the spirit.
For the gastronomes the city equally offered a far reaching horizon.
Body and mind had both a lot to gain from it.

After the bumbling and trembling of the new arriver,
I settled to the city's fast beat, the euphoria, and the possibilities.
Often returning to my little island late at night,
Giddy with excitement and filled with a sort of fulfillment -
Looking forward to their bigger and more colorful doses.

Some nine years have passed since my forced exodus from Tulsa.
Nolan has grown on me with its complex trappings,
And I now feel satiated with the city life and the invisible
Seeds of change in me have turned into discernable sprouts, announcing
I could not continue in the city, I must move on.

The excitement of the city, I began to discover,
Did not add up to happiness – it only lead to wanting more excitement.
It began becoming clear to me that I could not build the edifice
Of happiness with excitement alone, some deeper connections
With life were required for its construction.

Nolan did not create permanent friendships,
As people were always running with an invisible gun on their heads.
Neither could I attach myself to a woman who had little time to
know who I was.
The earlier years of excitement now echoed with hidden loneliness –
A child's emptiness after a day at a carnival.

A drug can not give a permanent solace to the searching mind,
Just as excitement and entertainment can not satisfy our deeper inner urges.
Environment for mind must be open, free, and un-distracting,
To allow a fine plant to breathe, which also needs its own space and
nourishment.
Neon lights, blazing colors, and chemical triggers can not touch the soul.

In a city no one is happy,
Each pads his unhappiness in his own way.
To the mentally ill, add the alcoholics, drug addicts, and insomniacs –
The city stands quite a bit on its legs due to a spectrum of
medications.
It represents some sort of defiance of nature – and pays for it.

Man's ability to take care of himself is impaired in a city.
You absorb the city but the city never absorbs you.
A city does not give but it sells.
Even with its panache and energy, enticement and entertainment,
There lurks beneath the city a quiet, steely, stubborn loneliness.

You wonder at first why it should be so -
Where is the crack in the glitter?
God created the village in a flash of thought,
To give man an environment to be absorbed in,
But man created the city to absorb it.

In a city you feel moved by a gunpoint,
Forcing you to be focused on the task ahead,
Not on the voyage of life.
Everything moves with its own rhythm,
Preventing the symphony of life to take place.

You look at the city children
And see how commerce has robbed them of playgrounds.
They play and frolic at cul-de-sacs
And on concrete patches called parks.
You wonder how they will grow up.

In the buses and subways people avoid each other's eyes,
Not out of shyness but diffidence to communicate,
Set in by long solitariness and trepidation of the other person.
In apartment buildings people socialize in elevators, hallways, and
laundry -
Never revealing themselves, never truly becoming friends.

I have packed my belongings
And decided to return to my roots in Tulsa,
To live a freer life, closer to God, closer to man.
For man his life is to discover his soul and live with it -
For that he does not need to build skyscrapers.

I want to feel the unsmooth, soft earth below my feet,
See the uncluttered horizon in full width,
Be an element of my community,
Know my neighbors' first names,
And visit my grandparents' graves.

Many Splendorous Faces Of Eternity

The day has just begun its triumphant march:
Imperial, rough-shod, crusading.
Its ambitions touch a pinnacle, its mood heroic.
Its commonplace beginning an unintended deception.
In a deft sleight of hand it quantum jumps to its
Brilliant power, melting into frenzied fury,
Maturing into unfocused drunkenness.

A day raids while an evening seduces.
Its mood of grand opulence is inhuman.
It seems to challenge Gods.
Man makes most of day's immense attributes:
Light and heat.
Which uplift his mood to achieve things and massage his ego.
Day's bold and brutal reign lingers on
To dissolve into the mystical grandeur of a sunset.

A sunset is an erroneous appendage to a day,
As it has its own character, beauty, and message.
It is meditative, humble, and human.
Its fleeting existence on the horizon
Is dramatic, mystifying, and thought provoking,
Making us think of God, renunciation, other worlds,
Mystery of nature, and transitoriness of life.

Evening has tiptoed invisibly at the end
Of day's relentlessly furious reign.
Gods pitied man and created the evening,
To balm him, to calm him.
Evening has style, charisma, and serene seductiveness.
It has nothing to announce
But to invite us to an enchanting dance.

Its soothing and romantic transition between
Day and night has given it a place of its own.

An expectant relaxedness, pregnant enthusiasm drapes the mood,
Let aside are material projects and human problems,
Turned off are engines of intellectualized introspection.
Evening seduces man to seek the moment at hand,
To feel the pulse of life, to feel intoxicated,
So it seems there was no yesterday and there will be no tomorrow,
That transience of man is permanent.

In night you enter a different world,
So alien to morning, day, and evening.
Its smooth sensuous serenity is a transforming grandeur,
Its tranquility and dreaminess a supreme elixir
For the daytime stained spirits.
Day raids but night occupies.
Windows to heavens are opened
And for a brief period one thinks that there
Are other worlds besides ours.

Even more removed from the worldly life
Than an evening, night lets one remove
The covers of survival and fear and see
God at a closer proximity.
It is not a mood of gloom,
Not even the resurgence of hope,
But something beyond all that.

Have you seen a night sky in full bloom?
Iridescent with a billion brilliant stars,
Pointing to nature's opulent oeuvre,
Its magnificent magnitude and transcendent timelessness.
Universe liberates us
And gives us a special status
Because of our ability to comprehend it -
Harnessing many responsibilities on us.

The seemingly impregnable mystery of night is
Wilting to the enigmatic twilight of the pre-dawn.
Hesitant fragile hopes are dampened by the just-born fears
Engendered by the grayish halo wrapping the scene.
In about an hour the predawn morphs to dawn
As the intensity and volume of light increase.
In dawn's halo everything looks touched in gold.

Diffident and lazy sunrays just graze the earth,
Something mysterious seems to be happening:
A curtain is rising on something.
The limpid tranquility of dawn is enthralling
But at the same time puzzling:
What does it mean?
We are part of a bigger picture.

First hesitant footsteps of sunrays congregate
To perform a mystic dance of light and shade,
Over the sea, over the ground, over the mountain peaks.
While the day raids and the night possesses,
Dawn caresses without touching.
Its shimmering shyness alluding to something
Great and bold, something unique and transcending.

The chariots of morning have now arrived,
Noiselessly and invisibly.
The whole earth seems in a state of awake dreaming,
But still tranquil and mysterious; possessed and in control.
The dreamy majesty of the morning has tinged everything
With ethereality and silence, grace and beauty,
Elegant aura pregnant with obeisance to eternity.

Morning holds man in reverence of what is beyond this world.
It is a door to higher level consciousness:
Which is higher awareness, higher unity with nature, higher tranquility.
The dream to realize a more fulfilled life is possible,
If we take courage to enter the door of the morning
And walk to the horizon of eternity.

Eternity is within grasp if we break our shackles with the world.
Sublime tranquility of morning is a gift of God to man,
To keep his balance in the raucous turbidity of the day,
In the man-made insanity of the world,
To remind him that the doors of heaven are not yet closed on him.
God takes but God also gives.
The pristine glory of morning will remain forever the same,
To elevate the spirit and liberate the soul.
Morning is one of the splendorous faces of eternity.

Driving On I-84

I am driving on I-84 from Suffern, N.Y. to Andover, Mass.,
The 230 miles journey I often take to see my friends:
Bhans, Qazis, Tikkus, and several Kauls.
I feel troubled by the fear I may have missed some,
But the thought that many KPs don't read poetry comforts me.
They spend their leisure time in *katha-batha* –
A searing and raucous communication,
Heavily spiced with gossip – not a conversation.
KPs basically believe in only in two things:
Survival and *naniya-batta*.
Cultural activities are only an excuse for socializing.

Shortly after the start we pass over panoramic River Hudson,
While crossing the three mile Tappan Zee Bridge,
A idyllic body of water reminiscent of the great lakes in Adirondack.
Twenty-five miles down we surf on boulevard-like I-684.
We pass by Greenwich, the oasis of the rich.
At fifty-three miles we leave N.Y. and set foot on I-84, in Connecticut –
The diminutive state known for its day-time raiders of Wall St.
And artists using it as a tax shelter.

I-84 is not as renowned as some of its flamboyant siblings.
It is short, un-grand, narrow, tortuous,
And passes through un-famous towns and villages.
Everything around it seems small-scale.
But it is its common humanity that binds us to it.
In Connecticut it passes through a string of towns suffixed by "bury:"
Danbury, Southbury, Middlebury, Waterbury.

Passing Danbury, on Exit 7, we are reminded of
The huge reservoir, Candlewood Lake.
Waterbury rooftops, shopping mall, and church spire
Stretch zoom on horizon due to its skewed terrain.
Here we often stop at McDonald's.
In another twenty minutes we reach Hartford,
The mid-point of our journey.
We zip bypass the commercial center.
Just before it we see an exit for Asylum St.
And never fail to be reminded of George Bernard Shaw's saying:
If there were men living on moon,
They would be using earth as their asylum.

Seeing the small places off the highway
One feels the footprints of God.
Here live people who say what they mean,
And mean what they say,
Though it may not come out right.
In big cities we see the big ego at work,
The vanity of vanities.

Moving from villages to big industrial centers,
Man became wealthier, worked more, and smarter,
But all at a substantial loss to his inner imperturbability and
Connection to the great unknown.
Today's man can go to moon
But will not walk across the street to help his neighbor.

Driving is tranquilizing.
As we drive we are lulled into our past,
Even when the senses are on the road and the machine.
We go to our past because it is the only thing we really possess.
Other things are either transitory, illusionary, insubstantial,
insignificant,
Or belong to others.
Past is our real myth
Through which we see the present and the future.
After some age we do not create anything new,

Everything is a rework of the old materials.
We go to our past like children go to their mother,
To be soothed and nourished;
We want to relive the great drama of our life.
Past is a an inexhaustible theater
From which we draw new meanings of life.
We often wonder why we took certain decisions in past.
This is not because we were wrong then but because we have changed.
Events may look different depending upon how we place the life-mirror to see them.
Life is an experience, not a rehearsal of something yet to come.

The journey of life is our song as well as its singer,
It is the destination as well as its roadmap,
It is the birth of life as well its death and immortality.
We get lost in search of happiness
Till we realize our anchorless state is the bedrock we were looking for.
In life there are no winners or losers,
As in the end we all arrive at the same threshold:
The opportunity to enter the door to liberation.

In today's life we spend a lot of time on highways;
But we drive toward something -
But our inner journey has no destination.
Man created destinations but God created only a journey -
The journey of life.
"If the doors of perception were cleared
We should see everything as it is - infinite."*

katha-batha: an idle small talk
naniya-batta: a high quality meal

* William Blake

On The Way To Eternity

I am only moments away from dying;
The long journey of my life is ending with nature's scintillating precision.
Luckily I am still able to think.

I want to know if I conducted myself alright
In the reasonable and unreasonable responsibilities that are harnessed
on human life -
A drama more complex than any writer or philosopher has ever been
able to capture.

Beyond the discharge of responsibilities
There are the questions of heart and mind:
Did I live with passion for God, nature, intellect?
Did I achieve something good?

I was inspired by nature's order and principles
But found human beings inconsistent,
While intellectualism was not always helpful in living
And cultures moved too slowly.
Art was a good solace for the wounds of life,
But not for every wound.

I do not know if I wiped every tear I could have wiped,
I do not know if I have been fair and honest with fellow human beings,
I do not know if I worked to the best of my potential.

My long tyranny of thinking compels me,
Even at this special moment,
To sum up what I believe in.

I believe that man is a special creation of nature,
Who is unsuited for some extant social, religious, and legal strictures.
He comes with freedom that should not be abridged –
In fact an evolved society would try to enhance it.

Zealotry for money, fame, and religion are chains;
Good actions are important but good thoughts are even more important;
'I believe in the brotherhood of mankind and the uniqueness of the individual.'*

As I see at this precarious point between my life and after-life,
I think I did not achieve much.
Most of my best moments have been spent
In observing nature and man,
And thinking about them,
And writing a little bit on them.

I did not achieve any high positions in my profession and in society,
I did not gain any fame whatsoever,
I did not amass any significant wealth.
I feel sorry for the creditors,
As they will lose a lot on me,
When I am gone.

People did not like me
Because they saw me too arrogant and independent,
Selfish and shallow.
As a result I gathered only a few friends,
Pushing me deeper in the cocoon of my loneliness.

My life hangs at the mercy of a fair assessment,
But I am serene and ready to go to the next life.
I am betting my entire past on the glory of my future.

I am ready to be dissolved in the vastness of cosmos,
Broken into subatomic particles,
Without a name,
Without an address,
Without the shackles of thinking.

Give me a flower,
Give me a letter -
Your message to Eternity,
While I still have a few moments to live.
On my behalf I will tell it
That human beings on earth,
Living in the present Technology Age,
Strut and fret much,
Without carrying a lot of joy in their hearts.

* A. Einstein

A Reflection From The Mirror Of God

I have been driving long and hard,
Over the tortuous, rugged terrain.
The struggle was occasionally relieved
By splendid, seductive scenery on the way.

During the journey many times I thought of quitting,
As the prize did not seem worth the perspiration and the anguish.
But the drive to continue was unrelenting.
Its insane impulse was as troubling
As it was mysterious.

Now I am within the euphoria range of my destination -
My home – my answered prayers –
The essence of my existence.
My road is finally ending.

Stepping inside the home
I was shocked and dazzled
To see a cosmic glow all around,
Suffused with a hypnotic music,
Ensconcing me to a permanent dream,
And around me angels danced with magical rhythms.

There was nothing in the home now
Like the way it used to be.
I wondered if I could live here anymore.
But gradually I realized that
I was in the other-world
And would not be returning to earth.
I was now in an imperishable home,
Immersed in a new consciousness.

In my new home there is no beginning and no end -
Everything is eternal.
There are no desires and there are no thoughts,
No success and no failure.
I experienced a revelation
That everything in cosmos is
A reflection from the mirror of God.

The Meaning Of Love

The meaning of love could be found in stars,
But one does not have to go that far;
The value of love could be plumbed in the depths of one's soul,
But one does not have to go that deep.

The power of love is felt in the heave of one's heart,
Its beauty in the mystery of the relationship between the two lovers,
Its music in the silences punctuating their communications.

Love is truth
And truth is beauty,
Together love, truth, and beauty
Weave the fabric of
Human soul, consciousness, and cosmos.

Love breathes immortality at every point,
It transcends consciousness and world.
It is the ultimate idea
Which carries human beings to God.

Love is a song as well as its silence,
It is a vision as well as its impossibility,
It is a dream as well as its death.

It Rained In Rockland Yesterday

It was only yesterday that we had a rain over Rockland,
An inundation without reservation, without inhibition.
Every rain drop raced after the next as if in an eternal chase;
Getting closer but never achieving the target.
The outpouring was an immense waterfall,
Happening apparently without reason.

The concatenation of rain drops produced a drilling staccato,
Piercing into the labyrinthine recesses of brain.
Awareness was not lost but one sensed to be
Transported to a different world.
Earth felt soft and time quivered.
The worldly structures receded beyond apprehension.

Standing behind the kitchen-deck door I saw
A miracle happening in front of my eyes:
A vast congregation of parachutes descending
From an unknown origin, for an unknown mission.
Each rain drop had an urgency in its fall,
An enigmatic pregnancy in its form.

Water squished and splashed on the ground,
Gushing into the old grooves, filling the nooks and crannies.
It sheet-spread over the lawn with gay but reckless abandon,
Sweeping across the careless contours,
Drenching the tree roots lying above aground,
And gushing into the streamlet bordering our property.

A rain is more than a condensation of vapor,
Or a nourishment much needed by vegetation,
Arid lakes, and depleted rivers.
It quenches the parched human spirits,
Balms the worldly wounded,
And breathes in a whiff of the other luminosities of universe.

Rockland is a supine, sober bedroom of New York City.
Bereft of its glamour and clamor.
A town neglected and despised in the
Elite shadow of Manhattan.
A metropolis raids but a village submits.
Humans still put on their best face in small places
But in large cities they try to be what they are not.

The rain in Rockland is a celebration of the unknown:
In Manhattan it is an inconvenient intrusion.
A city takes more than it gives,
Though it appears the other way
Due to its seductive shimmering sheen.
It molests the fine nature of man
Through his prurient weaknesses.
The world excites but nature soothes.

Yesterday, it rained through the Kashmir in me,
Bringing out the echoes of my childhood:
Streaming din of cricket games played in courtyard;
Getting drowned for days in tragic feelings watching a Dilip Kumar movie;
Imagining romance with the neighborhood girl Zoon,
Which our religious divide forbade;
Discovering the first saplings of the grand loneliness taking root in me.

In A Woman's Bosom

She emerged from the azure and tranquil waters of the lake:
Awash, dripping, glimmering, satiated.
Her physical aura was lustily sanguine,
Her beauty limpidly transparent.
It seemed she had come to the lake for an interlude of fun,
Not in any tiredness with the world,
But with a vision of having a romance with herself.
That is an aspect of woman:
Self-involved, controlled, sensuous, romantic.

God created man and woman in different images,
To satisfy the design of life.
Man is an outsider but a woman has roots in earth.
Man is a challenger and a searcher,
Woman is an absorber and a nurturer.

Man likes to explore,
But for woman everything is a rediscovery of herself.
A woman is what she is
But a man is what he would like to be.
A child is his mother's extension
But is his father's reflection.
Woman possesses but man occupies.

In love woman does not give herself to man
But absorbs the man within herself,
While man gives a part of himself to woman.
So when love breaks woman feels empty
But man feels diminished.
Woman prays to God to absorb his message
While man prays to become His message.

Life is not divided between absorption and radiation,
Between being and becoming,
Between extension and reflection,
Between pregnancy and ambition.
But it is the synthesis of the two.

A woman endeavors to live within nature.
To her a lot of the architecture of politics
And business woven by man is irrelevant.
If it were left to her the world would be more peaceful.
Like a lake she is self-contained –
Her worldly circumference covers her universe.
While man raids, woman assimilates.

If man is the searing energy of sun,
Woman is the soothing shade of an evening.
If man is the creator of the world,
Woman is the relief from its excesses.

Time is still moist with woman's tears.
In a woman's bosom lie compassion and tenderness,
She is the long-awaited shore for her tempest-tossed lover,
A sane instinct for life over its destruction.
Woman's genius for living has yet not been appreciated –
She is a ray of light which has not yet been
Given a chance to illuminate.

But Alas The World Has Tied My Hands

Yesterday the sun shone bright in Rockland,
After many a chilly gloomy day.
The emergent but yet shaky spring danced over fragile but lithe new
blossoming.
There was a bounce in the air, there was springiness in the ground.
Everywhere I looked around there were colors of you,
Every blade of grass I touched resonated with your memory.
Longing to see you overpowered me so much
That I forgot that I am not free to see you.

My dear I wanted to share with you the difficulties I am in,
I wanted to let you know of the shackles around my hands –
Condemned prisoner that I am of this world.
I am being punished for my ancient sins.
But the doors of justice I have thumped on with all my might
Are still defiant to even open a wink.
I wish I could let you know all this,
But my thoughts are frozen, my lips are sealed.

I am walking through this world
But I feel I am not one of its inhabitants.
I see around me too much commerce but too little heart,
Too much calculation but too little value,
Too much information but too little vision.
I am surrounded with glitter and excitement but I am lonely.
How I wish I could talk or write to you but I have no time.

I would like to chase you out of the dens of my fears,
And draw you in the valleys of my dreams.
I want to hold you in the wings of my thoughts
And keep you warm with the dance of my breath.
I would like to live with you every minute of the day,

31

Till the last moment of time.
Our love could be brighter than Sirius,
More perfect than a full bloomed lotus in a tranquil lake.
But all this can not happen as
I am tied down in a long cultural incarceration.

The shades have been pulled down on the still smoldering ambers of
the day,
Evening has descended on earth in serene stealthiness,
The survival stresses of the day are melting into
A placid and romantic mood.
It seems that in spite of its many sharp angles, life is still worth living.
At this time I wish I could be with you,
But my angel we know that the world has the first claim over me.

I love you to the last atom of my being:
You are my invisible light, the essence of my meaning.
I have chased you through the cosmic uncertainty
But always believing one day you will be mine.
After eons now it seemed our tryst was close
But alas the world has tied my hands.

I may not meet you in this life
But I have absolute faith that in my next life
The world can not take you away from me.
I will call you in the cosmic stillness of dawn,
I will look for you in the ravishing sensuousness of the evening,
I will wait for you till the world frees me from its chains.

A Cup Of Tea

A cup of tea is a balm to the stressed life,
A replenishment of energy,
A change of mood.

What is the miracle in the marriage
Of tea leaves and hot water?
We only know that a splendidly tasting and aromatic
Mood-transforming brew emanates.

Civilization is woven in cups of tea.
Every effort, however ambitious,
Ends in tiredness and some disenchantment:
A cup of tea restores us to our primal vigor.

A cup of tea does not give a crashing euphoria
Or a seductive drunkenness
But stimulates a soothing state:
Palpable tranquility, sensuous serenity.
In a tea cup you see a different universe.

We have to squeeze a tea-break from
The clutches of high-stress life we live in,
We have to defeat the forces of our culture temporarily,
To create a moment for ourselves,
To continue our dream.

A cup of tea opens a door to another realm,
More settled than ours, more hopeful, more inspiring,
Where there are no rewards and no punishments.

Where a journey is more important than its destination,
A commitment is more significant than its culmination,
Success is less important than the resolve to achieve it.

A cup of tea is a joy forever,
A float in tempest-tossed existence,
A window on another world.

Seeing Through A Window

A window is a fine thing to have,
Whether inside or outside.
Looking is the primary function of mind,
Which may turn into seeing.
We see not only to find new and old things
But also to see nothing.
It is the nothingness that is more significant than the things.
Mind needs a reference to establish objectivity
And a boundary between the spiritual and the material.

A window is larger than us
Because it has purpose, objectivity, and selflessness.
For every clear window man has nine stained windows.
It is the message from nature (God) that we corrupt
That tangles our lives and turns them into a shadow unbleachable.
If we could only see clearly we would be riding an angelic horse,
Our journey here on earth would become a ribbon of light.

Have you seen a serene slice of nature
On a clear irenic day –
A tapestry of mystic pregnancy,
A trance waiting to happen now -
A communication connecting us with eternity?
Man and nature are the same but eons of misunderstanding
Has put between them an immutable wall.

Man has many distractions in the world.
Spun by culture, invented by commerce.
Petty materialistic toys offered easily ensnare him.
For every such tie man loses an equivalent spiritual freedom.
Problem is that material world is easy to understand

But spiritual world needs jettisoning of some of our pet assumptions,
values, and visions.
A window is a way to get out of ourselves,
To belong to the world beyond ourselves,
To feel that we belong to a much larger phenomenon.
Our stay on earth is but a twinkle in the cosmic dance.
Man is greater than his achievements, higher than his aspirations.

Man's journey has not been easy,
For each enlightenment there are two falsehoods,
For each brilliant vision there are two abysmal illusions.
But we must try to lift ourselves above the trashy daily worldly life.
Even if we fail to achieve the crest of human life's splendor,
We would still have gained some light, some freedom, some joy,
And some insight into the larger things.

Let us start with having an outer window,
And become good unbiased observers.
Then graduate to the creation of an inner window
(The two windows are connected)
And start seeing things that were not there before.
We will see a garden before us, beautiful and magnificent.
But it can disappear any moment if we do not hold on to it.

Sometimes I Think The Poetry Of Human Heart Will Never Die

Sometimes I wonder if any fine thing in life is enduring?
I have seen men of resplendent promise die
In the ravishing bloom of their youth;
I have seen great leaders of spirit
Obscured by patina of time.
History has buried magnificent artists,
And noble men disappear from man's thin memory.
Man's power is a twinkle in God's mood.

The glory of wealth can be grayed over
By one stubborn nasty stretch of market.
Political power snuffed out by a wicked election.
Popularity is a rickety pedestal
That can turn slippery with one scandal,
Or falling out of fashion.

Human body is a fragile gift of nature
That can crumble with one disease.
I have seen revolutions of just causes
Suffocated by inertia and ignorance of masses,
Choked to death by brute power of the elite.

Everything in life seems to be temporary,
Except the stupidity of man.
Why are we trying to make grand edifices on a bridge,
Why are we trying to change life to what it is not?
God's vision is written on every micro-event of life.
But grandeur of man's spirit glows in the infinite layers of time.

I often walk the evergreen path down the hill,
Which in each season wears a magical costume.
Tulips in spring raise their natty heads in solemn dignity
And the aristocratic aloofness of roses frames their iconic beauty.
The charismatic presence of a weeping elm seduces silently.
If there is any permanence in life, it is in these.

After the day's brutality we are soothed
By the delicate caresses of the evening,
Sublimating into the nirvana of the night.
In the evening we want to jettison the crassness of our ego
And the vulgarities of the world -
But we want to invite the charioteers of the spirit.
Art of living is in how we spend our evenings.

Let us usher in beautiful women to talk with
(Men are obsessed with their bodies,
Never exploring the sublimity of their spirits)
And bring smooth wine to galvanize our mood.
Let music embellish an inspired moment of life.
Let us smell the fragrance of earth
And absorb the romance of the Milky Way on horizon -
Let us dream for a while.

An evening is an hour of beauty,
Our connection with eternity.
It is the consummation of human consciousness
With all that is and that can be.
Life is temporary
But the beauty of God is infinite.
Sometimes I think the poetry of human heart will never die.

Elysium Of Loneliness

I am driving on George Washington Bridge on my way to home
After a grueling workday.
The traffic is torturous and my nerves are aching
For the relief of my home and the exuberant mood of wine.

Every weekday is a smothering grind of the outer world,
Just saved from a total disaster by the tapestry of my inner world.
Now living in my sixth decade I have seen a lot of life –
A lot of which I would not repeat.

I live 30 miles north of Manhattan,
In a rural mosaic of rivulets and strip-forests.
My sparse solitariness has been further augmented
By my wife's walking away from me on account of our dissimilarity:
We were like opposite-colored bishops on the chessboard of life –
Together but not with each other.
She was interested in cutting costs
While I was interested in cutting ties with the world.

My solitude is reinforced by my unpopularity among people -
Especially among women;
Which has saved me their endless chase through
The tinsel social scenes and happy-hour bars.
The punctuated absences of my two college-age children
Further helped me to create a world of my own.

People aspire for adulation and greasy ties with the world
But I have evolved into a serene loner, an ambitious romantic.
I found that wealth and popularity were shimmering illusions:
They take in more than they give.
For me a single rose can make a garden.

The world is afraid of loneliness
But there is no loneliness
If you give yourself to your inner space.

I often hang around on my deck
To slice my gaze through the profusion of trees
Embroidering the backyard.
Out yonder where the tree-tops mingle with
The diaphanous azure veil of the skies,
I hear footsteps of God walking in eternal silence.

Shakespeare said ripeness is all:
Solitude is ripeness.
We do not want to bounce and scream
Walking on the trampoline of world
But see, think, understand, and absorb
The ever mysterious pulse of life.

I visit Rainrock, a small forest ten miles from home.
I walk through the high-density space
Where light sneaks through trees
And sky is a patchwork mosaic above.
Hours pass and I do not get the fill.
Though bereft of humans there is no loneliness here -
One feels the company of something larger.

Out there in woods
I find the majestic serenity of God.
The elements of nature connect with my elements.
There are no messages but one of absorption
With the mysterious and eternal universe.
Its grandeur surpasses everything.

"Think me not unkind and rude
That I walk alone in grove and glen;
I go to the God of the wood
To fetch His word to men." *
Hours pass and I find myself immersed in books;

The voyage that never seems to end –
But its thirst never quenches either.

In the beginning - if there was one –
There was no loneliness;
Everything was in God's shadow
But when man created the world
His loneliness was born.

When my energy begins to sag
I put activities on hold
And prepare for the journey of sleep.
Entering its labyrinthine paths
And kaleidoscopic light-patterns
I feel I am touching the feet of eternity.
Between the day and night I do not know
Which is the more life-giving?

I go to shopping malls –
Not to shop but to see women and children
Wrapped in the ribbons of excitement -
Their lust for things unhinged.
I see how temporal happiness enthralls people
And sooner or later makes them lonely.

Days end and give way to the majesty of evenings,
And evenings subtly melt into the aura of nights.
Sleep reawakens our soul
And the eternal drama of life continues –
A vast symphony that seems to be conducted
By a consciousness higher than ours.

As I walk on the last few stretches of life
I feel the inherent grandeur in the conception of life.

* R.W. Emerson

Flowers

Cast against the blue sky
A flower is a figure with an aura of presence;
Its scintillating colors wrapped in gentle contours,
Sculptured with a spectrum of petals and a stem,
Forming an enigmatic shape -
A piece of human heart hanging for a moment,
But evocative of eternity.

Human heart looks for things which please it:
Images of desire echoing beauty, love, truth, God;
Immortality, transcendence, principles, reason.
A flower has all these and more.

A flower is a peep into the human heart:
Effervescent with longings for beauty and truth.
A flower never lies, it has no guilt to hide.
It is a longing frozen on the wing-tips of time;
It is a dream never realized,
But whose idea is immortalized in consciousness:
A memory whose residue echoes in the farthest recess of personal time,
An idea inscrutable in its meaning.

A flower is an icon and essence of our existence.
When we look at a flower,
We do not attempt to understand it –
We just experience it.

Dreams

In the beginning God created the dream,
Later both God and man created the world.

Eons later the dream has become the illusion
And the mind-created world the reality.
This confusion between illusion and reality
Has remained the dagger between what is given to us
And what we could make of it.

We do not prepare for our dreams,
But are lead into an inward journey
To a destination where we would like to go,
But did not intend to go.

Mind tries to convert all external reality to a dream.
The struggle between the two is the fabric of human existence.
It is the dreams which give us pain.
But if we shut off the dream,
The existence turns dry as dust,
And there is music no more.

A dream holds us strongly by its hand,
But reason commands coldly.
While intellect works by slow sequential steps,
A dream dances its way to the destination.

Works of reason are the jewels of human mind,
But the creations of dreams are both the works of logic and beauty.
Organized thought for too long may smother the birth of a new vision,
A dream has more power than a thousand reasons.

Life is a continuous inner dream
Smothered by reality.
We dream, we are awakened, we go back to the dream.

Maybe, it is all a dream,
The external reality but our own fabrication.

Peace

What is peace?
Is it a state of mind or a physical condition of existence?
It is more –
It is the particular structure of consciousness.

Man does not need peace to survive,
But it is the prerequisite for high level creative work
And the search for God, Beauty, and Truth.
And to hear the music of the universe.

Why should anyone invade someone's peace of mind,
It is as immoral as disabling someone.
Man comes with peace
But the world often robs it in wanton ignorance and crass cruelty.

Peace is a much ballyhooed weapon among the politicians,
Those who sloganize it the most know it the least.
Often a nation's peace is in the hands of debased politicians,
Who treat it as a commodity,
Often selling it for money.

Peace is a human right,
Which shall not be abridged, abrogated, or axed by anyone.

Man was sent by nature in peace,
He should live his transient life in peace.

BEAUTIFUL PAIN

Much as God made human life divinely beautiful,
He made Its passage through world sometimes painful,
As if to harden its mettle
For the eternal journey ahead.

Perspective Of Time

It was some six weeks ago that I met you accidentally at my cousin's place –
Twenty-four years since I glimpsed your face –
The face that seems to have a new emotion playing on its sculptured contour -
The contour that made you different.
Your eyes were still securely placed under the arches of the same wayward dense eyebrows,
But the dissipated restlessness and the dark ancient glint in them were entirely new.

I approached you with excited trepidation, pained wonder;
You recognized me with an electric but unsure gesture.
Crossing the distance between us with measured flippant steps,
Your right hand hooked my neck in a wild embrace,
While your withered mustache breezily rubbed my face.
We froze in that eternal silent union, till our speech rescued us from this strange moment.

Your face – the smooth monitor of your emotional world –
I found riven by the deep fault lines of pathos.
Its classic shape and sculpted features seemed smothered by strong sad experience,
The sparkle in the eyes was replaced with the dimness of distance and dismay.
The serene thoughtfulness and wonder had gone;
What was left was still smoldering ashes of an ancient fire,
Elegant ruins of a grand mansion.

Seeing you my life's checkered tapestry uncoiled,
Transporting me to the folds of our shared past –
Into the echoes of our histories;

To the nascent awareness burgeoning at the threshold of our young adulthood.
Concatenations of the past images coalesced into kaleidoscopic mosaics,
Breathing new life in the old joys and new vitality into the old pains.

In the inferno of our youth we were led to dream of an enchanted life:
Of ideals and caring, of beauty and daring, of truth and adventure.
There would be the causes to fight for and missions of justice to accomplish,
There would be inspiring challenges to meet and elevating work to perform,
Equality among people would be the norm and gender gap would go to permanent nap,
Freedom of man would be guaranteed and the peace in the world would be a cause to fight for.

We were buffeted by our innocence, propelled by our conscience;
Life appeared God's gift to us to create beauty and dream dreams;
The humankind was a community and its problems were our problems;
The current of life felt strong and the challenges before us were inviting.
Time ribboned out of its spool and all roads leaped to future;
We had the emotion to go ahead and seemed to possess a vision of our goals.

But the ways of the world soon unfolded their swooping arms,
Planting roadblocks in our projects.
There was much suspicion of our motives, much cynicism on our designs.
Soon our work looked tedious and our confidence started to wilt.
We lost the way to our dreams
And they haunted us with nightmares.

Why is human life so difficult,
Why are so many humans insensitive?
If God gave us capacity to dream,
Then why didn't He give us the resources to realize them?
The world has a long history, the human has come a long way,
But the strife for existence continues.

Much has happened all these years, much did not happen,
The irreversible arrow of the hallowed time made its ineradicable marks,
The transient blossoming of our lives withered on the way,
We paid the price for the shining spark of life,
Till the wreath we wore hurt us with its thorns,
For every joy we had, we paid twice in pain.

Life is a shining garden on the horizon,
For whose glory we are compelled to bleed.
It is a promise we must take unquestioningly.
A thousand times we fall on the way to Elysium,
But we must pick up ourselves and resume the enchanted journey,
We must not complain, as it is not the hero's way.

Today I look at your wasted face
And feel the perspective of time hallowing our lives.
I feel torn and ashamed that I could not do much to soften your misery.
We are a blip in the cosmic dance, invisible in the cosmic time,
What is man's life to the universe, what difference does our anguish make.
We are a brief spark in the blinding darkness,
Strewn planks of a ship wreck.

The Mercy Of Montessory Beach

There is something about today I do not know:
It is wildly quiescent, uneasily reposed;
The air is heavy and light laboriously languid.
My apparent malaise seems to have a deep
Wound supporting it – the placid mouth of
A turbulent volcano, gentle plumes of smoke
Fronting a caravan of gushing flames.

I have been traveling on this earth oven fifty years now
But the journey has never been smooth.
What is it, I often wonder, that is behind my melancholic vision,
Sorrowed immersion in life, asynchrony with its grand demands?
Why do I have to bleed often on the hallowed white sheen of life,
Pay twice with pain for every joy I have?

The doctor thought that I suffered from
A long childhood love deprivation,
That matured into the steel cage of
Gloom around me. Lying on the couch helplessly,
I thought that supposititious conclusion was emblematic of
Science's continuing ignorance of the interiors of human mind.

I was not a loveless child, nor inclined to low spirits.
My sorrow is a long story of my developing awareness of the
World that I gained, as I journeyed gingerly through its labyrinthine
alleys.
The world hidden by a million facades,
The world run by a million hypocrisies –
The paralyses of imagination, the corrosion of the human spirit.

Man is spinning the efficient wheels of technology –
Turning life into a cold clockwork.
But does that encourage the rapture of experience,
Enrich and expand consciousness?
Will the big business give us the big joy of living?
These things are for ease and not for soul.

The blazing goal of this civilization is to make money,
But people do not realize that materials do not
Connect well with the human spirit.
And without human spirit there is no meaningful life.
A temporary high can not a life make,
Nor can provisions against insecurity substitute happiness.

Sex is the big apple of the current culture,
Next to money the best thing man can have.
Nature did attach high pleasure with procreation,
But sensual pleasure can not be the driving force of life,
As it has a week mental coefficient,
Making it narrow, fixated, and unsustainable.

Like the galaxies in the deep space,
Everyone in today's culture is running in a drunken frenzy.
They do not know what they are running away from,
But they know they are running to the next thing to do.
There is too much passion, without reflection,
Which boils over, creating emptiness, evolving into a void.

Come Love let us leave this world together,
For here we have endured a million pains,
Our spirits suffered a million insults.
Our past is a mosaic of our failures and fierce courage,
Our present a windblown string of fragile pendant hopes,
Future looks to be a concatenation of everyday lives.

Lord made human life capable of rewarding spiritual experience,
Studded with a high potential for creativity.
The short journey was meant to be
A celestial dance over the worldly abyss,
Broken now and then to help the unfortunate fellow humans,
And offer obeisance to nature.

But from Lord's conception to man's execution,
Many foreign and strange elements intervened,
Making a mockery of the original blueprints.
Looking at the potential of human life
And the actual work accomplished,
The mind recoils and the heart feels stabbed.

The material greed of man is limitless.
When and how it contaminated human life is obscure,
But once having found its root, it has been
Virtually impossible to get rid of.
Instead of stemming its wildly poisonous growth,
Modern man has lavishly built on it.

Today's man celebrates his freedom endlessly,
Thinking he has created a new spirituality.
His illusions are deep, his salvation will take ages.
The present reign of darkness will stay long,
Till one day an avatar will be born to
Free him from the shimmering bondages and give him real freedom.

Why should we live wounded and withered,
Why should we stain the chalice of nectar we came with?
(Sin has no size – the little sin is equal to the large sin)
Why should we sleepwalk at noon,
And be in continual stupor?
Come Love let us leave this world together.

I can not be compressed any more with my worldly woes,
So I have to find relief in the seascape of Montessory.
Here I see the pulsating froth of the sea waves –

Timeless sentinels of freedom that we came with but lost to the world.
Montessory vacuums out my poisons and lofts me in the direction of
the horizon.
I feel unburdened at the moment and free to move in any direction.

The mirth and frolics at the beach, the skinny freedom, the
beckoning horizon,
Conspire to change the stage of life. Away from the Wall Street cannibalism,
Distant from the political shenanigans, cut off from the insane man-
made stresses,
The buffeting beach breeze buoys the trammeled spirits to live,
Frees the long repressed desire to be an element of nature.
The mercy of Montessory Beach is immense.

She Has Changed

July has injected a delirious torpor in me,
Spinning off a drunken state of lassitude.
What to do, where to go?
In the throes of frozen energy Montessory Beach beckoned.
Forty miles of drive was an easy bargain
To unload my burdens, to thaw my stifled joy.

Montessory Beach is a full clean horizon
Melting into a pulsating sapphire blue ocean,
Fringed by a glimmering golden sand beach.
The bosom of the surf is ample and its lust high.
The sea birds garland the scene
And the maverick breeze caresses
In a frivolous yet searing romance.

I look around to see happy bodies lying on the beach,
Urging the stressed minds to unwind,
To salute the god of nature,
To give all to the magnificence of the moment.
This transportation to the other world
Has created a nirvana-like state.

Looking at nature's frame around human life,
I wonder if we can not get from life what we want
Then how good is it?
The potentials of life are greater than life itself.
I want something because it is there,
Let reason play its elegant games.
We glorify life so much
That it becomes a barrier to our fulfillments.

Intoxicated with my new upliftment
I scanned the beach for the worldly elements.
To my shocking surprise I saw Emily,
Someone I knew twenty-five years ago,
Relaxedly lying scores of bodies away from me.
My stunned senses had to work twice hard to confirm that.

Emily and I schooled in Columbia Engineering.
She an organized, hard working student,
I a dreamy world-disenchanted mind,
Trying to find a foothold in the slippery universe.
She knew what she wanted, I did not know where I was going.
We lived planets apart
But there was a mysterious magnetism pulling us together.

The sojourn at Columbia was nearing its end
Yet we did not know what we should
Make of our romantic friendship.
I thought if we lived together for the rest of our lives,
It would be a cool connection,
Amorous and worldly-wise.
But she was a creature of the world,
I a follower of the spirit.
There was no congruence of our universes.
She did not understand our differences
And thought I was selfish and lacked commitment.
She wanted to stay but I did not know how.

Our parting was a tranquil mourning,
Goodbye silent so-longs.
After a momentary mechanical embrace
We tore away and walked in our directions.
But only after two minutes on our roads
We stopped and turned around to see each other again,
To feel the still smoldering fire between us,
The echoing power of what might have been.

Emily's sudden appearance ignited
The powder-keg of my memories,
Momentarily disturbing my new-found serenity.
Though we had broken physically
I had maintained a spiritual connection with her:
She was not like me but she loved me.

Twenty-five years later
I saw an Emily more confident and poised than before.
Her ebullient beauty was intact,
Her elegant coiffure in place,
Though a little loose and gray.
But her manner was casual businesslike.
Gone were her mischievous banter and
Her faraway romantic drop-dead smile,
Care creases punctuated her now austere face.
And she treated me as an interesting old acquaintance.
Her half-contemptuous smile on my other-worldliness
Sneaked out of her usual social control.

She told me that after our breakup
She suffered more than two years of loneliness,
Rescued finally by her sense of survival.
She married a wealthy day-time trader and had two children.
She lives in middle class security and self-consciousness,
A regular churchgoer and a community activist,
And continues to work as an engineer.

I looked in her eyes and found a stranger,
Hanging precariously from the hoary cliffs of my past.
Our joint history had become a legend,
Love naturalized into benign fossilized crystals of memory.
Time had dilated our intimate space
And our universes had further drifted apart.

She wanted to know what I had done.
I did not know how to tell her that
I was still a dreamy drifter dancing on the outer

Edges of existence: a rolling stone incapable of gathering moss.
I was a loner who had ultimately found a tiny threshold
In the colossal emptiness of the universe.
I was a worldly failure living by the brilliance of the stars.
How could I tell her that I had not changed?

As it became unbearable to be with Emily any longer
I tore myself from her in an abrupt, rude detachment.
I half-ran across the beach to the parking lot,
And drove home in wounded agitation,
Grated by the thought that
While I had maintained my platonic love for her,
She had discarded me in the dustbin of the world
As a miserable loser, an irredeemable lost soul.

But over time I found solace in the knowledge that
Montessory Beach's hospitality
Is eternal and without recrimination.

Who Am I ?

Often in the heat of living
I revisit the old question:
Who am I?

Through the beautiful and the ugly of life,
Through the joyful and the painful of life,
Through the victory and the defeat of life,
Through the probing of the cosmos,
The one question that has remained unanswered is:
Who am I?

Intuitively it seemed I should be one of the following:
A creation of God, who is passing through human form for the
training for a higher state of being;
A highly evolved specimen of nature whose reach and grasp is wide and high,
Who can make a large difference in the quality of human life on earth;
A manifestation of God who has come to earth to do some specially
great things;
An agglomeration of experiences, ideas, desires, physical entity, and goals,
Whose viability depends on nature and chance;
A being which transcends human understanding.

But I would not accept my intuition on its face value,
So I set myself to answer this eternal question.
I went through the innermost recesses of my being,
I went through every event of my history I could remember,
I went through every pore of my body
And the minutest sensation I could fathom.
I went through every element of science I know,
I walked through all the religions that I have explored.
I also went through all the folklore and mythology that I have come across.
I roamed over all the literature that I had absorbed.

After my sweeping and penetrating quest that I made in search of myself,
I found that there was nothing like myself:
It was a vast misunderstanding.
The addiction to self is deeply pervasive.
I was shocked that the myth of self that I had been harboring
In my bosom for all my life was the greatest illusion I have had.
Who am I?
Nothing but a superficial worldly reference –
Irrelevant to inner human life, irrelevant to cosmos.

A Leaf Falls

Up on the top of a fall colors decked tree a solitary leaf holds itself in serene majesty.
The riotous colors dressing the entire maple tree are shocking and seductive.
Little did the tree know in spring and summer one day it will be raided by an army of colors,
Transported to another realm and stunned into an exotic appearance.
Does it know that its symphonic gaiety will soon be over and it will go through
The ignominy of nudity for several month long winter interlude?

Fall is the consummate of all seasons as it mirrors the human personality.
It has the flaming splendor, tantalizing exuberance, and gay abandon;
But it also has the sadness and stillness, shyness and reclusiveness of a human being.
Behind its robust grandeur lie the fault lines of the impending doom of the approaching winter.
Fall is an irony written in a climate, a verse of nature enigmatic and still eloquent.
Spring announces itself with a shriek, summer a loud mirth, but fall is a melancholy wrapped in a celebration.

In the beginning was God, who later gave birth to nature -
Before man came and before his intellect evolved.
For millions of years the mystery and power of nature awed man
But as science emerged nature receded from his mind.
Today it is just a mystic, grey background to man's existence:
Ununderstandable, un-connectable, inhuman.

Fall or spring, summer or winter, each has unique spirit and style, beauty and charm.

Nature's seasons are the backdrop to human existence: inalienable and indispensable.

Without the colossal majesty of nature around us we would not be what we are.

It is the nature we deny in us that haunts us in endless ways.

Technology has helped humanity greatly but it has no humanity in it.

The leaf at the top of the hallowed tree falls to ground but no one cares to look at it.

Why Do I Keep My Lonely Ways?

You ask me why do I keep my lonely ways.

The nature in me longs to come out of the convoluted depths,
To reconfigure my life, to enrich my mind.
I am an element of nature seeking the grand experience –
But there is an array of forces fighting the elemental urge.

Heart asks for peace, justice, and brotherhood;
Mind sees them as fitting architecture of ideas to live by.
But the world is soaked in greed, blindness, and ignorance.
It suffocates the grand visions of mankind;
It sows war, falsehood, strife;
It corrupts pure, natural impulses;
Replacing them with narrow earthly concerns.
It supplants natural freedom with material cages;
Poetry with petty survival wisdom.

Another human is a reflection of existence.
Human relationship is a door to liberation,
But culture and world has turned it into a functional tie,
Laced with selfishness and insecurity,
A mirror of the inner disorder and turmoil.

We live in a world of insane goals;
Of acquisitions, ego, power;
An existence woven in hollow, tinsel strands;
A life punctuated by mad, pointless rush.
Success is designed to curb, not liberate;
Manic economic competition sours our soul toward the fellow
human.

You ask me why do I keep my lonely ways.

Soul Of The Modern Man

In our hyper-convoluted, super-charged, and un-symbolic life
There is not much respite from the perversity of the world.

When the spirit sags the world prescribes a set of fixes:
The most popular is a to-do procedure, mechanical in nature:
Keep busy with anything and let the time go -
A soulless remedy to a spiritual malaise.

Life comes naturally with passion and glow,
Imprinted by nature for it to survive.
Man has made the world such that
In many cases it tramples these.

In today's world you try to keep away from others,
Lest they see through your façade and emptiness.
We run around meaninglessly for good amount of time,
Till tiredness forces us to sit and then we wonder on the
Insanity of running in the first place.

Amassing money is the chief value of our lives –
Though never knowing what to do with all of it.
The illusion that money equals happiness is the
The cruelest dagger that has penetrated the modern culture.

People endlessly acquire material things thinking they
Are building a grand edifice of joy and contentment.
But when the edifice is found to be vacuous and weak it collapses
At the first heartbreak the world gives, everything looks futile and
meaningless.

Mechanical pursuit of sex is another vaulted value of our times.
Its power lasts for sometime but it can never satisfy a man's soul.
In spite of its illusory nature greed is a supremely powerful elixir,
Like evil it is born again and again endlessly.
Loneliness, the invisible environment of our times,
Remains often hidden under the shimmer and clamor.
Our values, culture, work, and society contribute to it.
Man has yet not learnt to live with it and never will.

Modern man is tired and trapped, beaten and fearful.
He is stressed though still energetic. He is intelligent
But uninspired. He is healthy but not happy.
For he has tampered with his nature in blindness and greed.

The Nature Of Man

Trapped in the depth-less vortex of his making,
Man has cut off himself from the infinity –
The grand cosmic architecture.
A splendid aberration of his mental-machine.

He has traded his freedom to the worldly-order,
Stressed his tranquility and harmony by material progress,
And perturbed communication with the unbounded
By corporeal concerns.

Man is born free -
An animal designed to soar,
But a lofty creature grown remote to his nature,
A casualty of his survival myopia.

Man must live with nature in accord,
And with man with respect and love.
Peace and freedom are the same things,
If he should live in grandeur.

The rights of man are given to him not by man,
But they come from the kingdom of nature,
For it is in the nature of nature
To give each being and thing an inviolable space and form.

Man's freedom is his origin and existence,
His wholeness the condition of his cosmic identity.
The worldly order ought not take away what he has come with,
The worldly wisdom ought not stain his pristine primordial grandeur.

Child is a man displaced in time, but more helpless,
Let man protect saplings before dreaming of trees,
A child is a mirror of nature, a man its adulterated extension,
He should discharge his debts to nature before he weaves his agenda.

Man is his own message,
Tinkering with his nature is perilous.

Is That What Is Human Life?

Eyes unhappy to focus deeply on anything,
Legs performing their duty nonchalantly,
A pulsating shadow of pain in torso,
Body fighting to leave behind a harsh day's fatigue,
Mind restaging its arsenals to combat a spiritual wearying,
A gallant beginning in the morning is fading dismally,
A day in human life is ending.

Day in and day out human life
Must go through the rough worldly grind.
Human spirit must percolate through the jagged sieve
Before it can dream of glory.
Each emotion must be expended to survive,
Each thought committed to keep out of troubles.

An inflamed spirit, a sublime soul, an inspired mind,
Experience the sharp angularities of the world –
Its crassness, its insensitivity, its unsophistication.
We must fall in mud before we can look up at the stars,
A moment of bliss is entwined with a thousand miseries,
We must die a thousand times
Before we are toughened enough to hold a faith.

The world moves like a clockwork.
Each person aspires for power,
Each person pursues material goals.
Happiness and acquisitions are considered the same.
The ensuing insecurity is bottomless,
The mirage of happiness is chasing an ever receding horizon.

Human life is wasted in its daily chores,
Progress of worldly life a blinding illusion.
To make a house on the bridge of life
Is the most perverse plan.
What is spiritual in essence
Can not be secured in a material edifice.
I fall on the craggy edges of life
And ache with seething pain.
I tremble and murmur:
Is that what is human life?
I wonder if God had meant that we live the way we do,
Or is it our illusion, our fallacy?

I look through my window
At the verdant sheen outside,
Speckled with the majesty of trees touching the zenith,
I see the sinuous curves of a rivulet on the horizon,
I feel the infinite and the resplendent blue of the sky.

When the mosaic of colored leaves
Dance down to ground in fall,
Uncovering the stark and inner beauty of trees,
They point to the spirit behind,
The master's invisible hands.
Never at rest,
Never far away from human perception.

Aloft a silent salubrious evening,
Gliding over its serene mystery,
Rests the spirit of eternity,
The call of the unknown.
A point of light in the darkness,
Masked often by the material world.

When you recede from the world
You walk into the lap of nature –
The eternal mother.
It has beauty, principles, and truth.
You become nature when you give yourself to it.
It is a life where all the quests end.

Walking The Last Footsteps In The World

Today the resplendent morning tore off itself from the dark annular rings of the night,
While the birds were still half asleep in their vulnerably fragile nests.
I scrubbed myself close to remove the last vestiges of dirt reaching my new world.
A sparkling white shirt seemed best attuned to the occasion;
Deep blue denim I thought should drape the still soldierly legs,
Who are keen to carry the body in the one last salute to life.

Still waking up from the mists of the morning dream,
I feel eager to shake the last hand,
To say my last good bye,
To take my last walk in this world.
At moments I feel bristling with happiness,
Which seems to be rocking me off my balance.

For a long time the world was playing games with me
But unable to carry the charade any more I decided
To reject it outright and come out clean:
To secure my vision of life, to save my soul;
To send a message to fellow human beings
That it is better to suffer than be duped.

For every hope I became pregnant with,
I paid twice in pain in its miscarriage by the conditions of the world;
For every altruistic project I launched,
I paid twice in dejection by its rejection by the Wall Street;
For every dream that enkindled in me,
I paid twice in suffering in its shattering by the "real" world.

Why are we unfurling the false flags
Of materialistic achievements?
Why are we celebrating the victory
Of man against nature?
Why are we saving ourselves from pains,
While our whole community is inundated with them?

Falseness is more alluring to the world,
As it has more style to it, it is easier;
Excitement is more in demand than serenity,
As it delivers instantly and entails less investment;
Materialism looks more secure than spiritualism,
As it seems more real and takes less time to acquire.

Peace, inner and outer, seems to be a heavier intangible,
While today's world would rather like to work on more concrete
matters;
Happiness seems to be an abstruse concept of philosophy,
Which should be substituted by the more real aimless life.
Like in Quantum Mechanics we have accorded our difficulties
In reaching the truth the status of reality, thereby shortchanging our
understanding.

When one sees beauty in the spectral dance of a sunset,
Or greatness in the sacrifices a Gandhi makes to gain independence
of his people,
Or commitment in a Einstein spending thirty years of his life trying
to unify the forces of nature,
One sees where man's essence lies:
The power of faith over just survival,
The magic of mind over just brain.

I have had my battles with falseness and materialism,
I have had frustrations with modern man's aberration in
Calling the moment as the life and what he can see as the truth.
But I do not have to go along with the fashions of the times.
I have given up my worldly wealth, honors, and securities,
And I am ready to walk my last footsteps in this world.

There Is No Time

The pink dogwood flowering tree
Has nearly touched my 2nd Fl. study window sill,
Tempting me to pluck a ravishing blossom
And embrace it with abandon.
The brook contouring our backyard
Is hosting the migrant Canadian geese,
Who are floating with majestic ease.
I should mingle with the elements of nature
And feel the magic of its impulse.
But I can not do so as I have no time.

Between the morning's beckoning
To action to the evening 's relief at the survival
From the daylong wrestling with the world
Lie corpses of a million dreams,
Mutilated states of a billion half-dead hopes.
The crushing vortex of the daily life
Has shred the spirit of life into smithereens.
The inner poetry and order incubating long
Want to control the stage
But survival takes the upper hand
And there is no time for the spirit to dance.

Mind has its brilliant logical constructs
And heart has its exquisite emotions
But it is the combination of the two
That produces moving art.
A DiVinci, a Rembrandt, a Picasso,
Is a prophet of life,
For he practices a creative impulse
And lives in blissful harmony.
But to find them in yourself

And to bring them to life
Needs work and time,
But there is no time.

The very ill and the destitute,
The victims of the social justice,
The crushed and the suppressed by the political tyrannies
Punctuate the human landscape.
Their agony and helplessness
Challenge our minds and drill holes in our hearts,
Beckoning us to repair and rehabilitate them.
The heart of the humanity is large
And we have the wherewithals for the work,
But we do not have the time.

Our bookshelves are brimming
With elegant works on
Poetry, fiction, biography, and history:
Works of fecund and artistic minds,
Bearing a lifetime of work.
Here is a garden of roses,
Magisterial and seductive,
A feast we can not refuse,
But our busy lives do not afford us
The time to absorb the experience.

Our relatives and friends are the
Flowers in the garden of our experience,
The rainbows in our skies.
But the technology age
Has dented the hub
That holds us together:
We have the strong feelings to be with them
But we do not have the time to do that.

The world is a minefield of
Religious, racial, and social tensions,
Which can blast anytime.

Our streets are still moist with blood
And our guns smell of the last fired bullet.
Bigotry and violence rule the world.
Come let us turn the tide
And restore God's work to its original design:
Blissful, tranquil, pristine, seamless.
But alas there is no time.

In the beginning God required
Man to work, pray, and love;
Eons later man invented commerce, politics, and technology;
Ego and greed followed incrementally.
Man wants to make more money to be happier
But by first trampling on the happiness he already has
And then shutting doors on grander and more durable happiness.
Technology has abetted man in his greed
And swollen his head to ignore God's work,
Leaving him little time.

Now human life is remote from God's vision.
It has lost its spiritual magic
And has become a thing,
A badge-number, a commodity, and a contract,
Negotiable at a material value.
Our spirit has turned to a stained mosaic,
A broken symphony.
God's tapestry needs restorative work.
We can open the doors of
Religion, reason, and art to do that
But there is no time.

VIGNETTES OF TIME

Time hangs like an eternal riddle over human life.
Always there, always silent.
It is neither with us nor against us –
But our companion at the moments of pain, struggle, and death;
As it is with us at the moments of achievement, love, and joy.
The spirit of man would remain unrealizable in the world without it;
For it imparts the spirit its temporal form, order, and flow.

Lana Takes Retirement

It was yesterday that my friend Alan told me casually
That his wife Lana had decided to retire.
Though Lana's retirement has been a conversation
Between us for the last few years,
Yesterday's news gave me a pained quiver -
Its abruptness transmitting a cool disturbance through the spine,
As deep within me I thought she would not have liked to retire,
Unless confronted with the absurdities of life.
But this logical supposition may be exactly
What was not in her mind when she decided to take the retirement.
Against life we are all bumbling adolescents.

There is no definition of wisdom as applied to the conduct of human life.
Every golden rule of life is subject to debate.
What is life? - or, what is valuable in it, has been
A question tossed to every generation to answer,
With varying answers and variable meanings,
Depending on whose interpretation is considered.

Why does anyone retire when a lifetime has been invested
In the pursuit and development of worldly work? -
When one does not know any other way to live.
These questions remain unanswered,
As life fights its easy understanding.

Lana spent eighteen years in the New Jersey school system,
Teaching rich kids languages and other fine subjects.
She found a strong bond with her work –
As she is inclined to form with anything she does with good reason.

Years of teaching sowed in her the seeds of seeing
The possibilities in the kids,
Which lay inherently in their nature -
Unexplored and underdeveloped.
Teaching also sometimes opens windows
In teachers' minds, on a different life, on a different world.

Replanting herself in Florida,
Lana is conjuring a different calm, painting a different scene,
Which may engender a state of mind
Conducive to writing –
A fragile but surviving emotion in her,
A subliminal ambition daring to leap out now for fruition -
A veiled agenda well hidden so long.

She thinks she can push to a comfortable proximity
Her sprawling family and get away from
The torment of a working life.
She wants to contemplate Florida's and her life's horizon.
(While Alan will count the coins
And measure up Floridian fair fannies,
Though he will be unable to stay in Florida too long,
Because of its philistine and vapid culture.)

Apart from all the dreaming which a retirement triggers,
Isn't it after all an assiduous planning of the ultimate retirement?
Isn't compartmentalizing and packaging of the last part of our lives
the ultimate hypocrisy?
Why should we try to change ourselves, change the way we know
best to live?
Why don't we accept the nature's agenda
And feel as a dancing bubble of protoplasm destined to burst,
Feel the nature in us and cherish the moment?

But the conventional drama of retirement
May hold the ultimate wisdom.
Human life can not be lived by facts only,
It is very much dependant on emotion and metaphor.

Man's worldly life is a rattling of a hollow tin can:
Confined, programmatic, materialistic.

Retirement creates an opportunity to get away from these and more:
It gives a taste of freedom though not necessarily freedom itself,
One can live in a cocoon and confine oneself to things close to one's heart,
Attempt to do things which were frivolous on world's watch,
Meditate on the mystery of human life
Or feel the curve of water below the sail-boat,
Write on the absurdities of life one experienced
And unabashedly espouse wisdom.

You can walk on a Floridian beach and smooth step into a reverie
On the bending horizon afar,
Contemplate the surface tension of water holding the sand below your feet,
Swim into your childhood,
Seeing new meaning in the old unsophisticated notions,
Try catching a rainbow without looking at your watch,
Put your head on a pillow of sand,
Transcending into sleep,
More refreshing than a walk through a fragrant, flowered meadow.

The possibility of reaching back to your roots which the world blocked,
The chance to be yourself and not become one of its programs,
The retirement does hold opportunities to liberate oneself from the
worldly cage,
To contemplate the universe, to enjoy the beat of one's heart.

Lana, you have done the right thing,
You are attempting to arrive at a liberation from the world.

What Will You Do When I Am Gone?

When the sky shines blue
And a tremulous and luscious breeze is afloat
And when an evening lifts up into an ethereal mood,
Do not think of me but pay homage to the majesty of nature,

When the intimations of spring steal through winter
And hope rushes and stands on insubstantial ground,
Delight in tomorrow to be,
Let faith cross the chasms.

Each daybreak is a faith that God thinks of us,
Each heartbeat is a tribute to His work.
Life is a boat sailing on the heaving bosom of nature,
Its glory is transcendent.

The churn of the day to day worldly turmoil
Is a distraction to the spirit of man.
Each worldly involvement is a moment lost
In the pursuit of the eternal.

Take the world in a detached way,
Never surrendering your freedom and peace.
Live for larger than life goals,
Keeping in view the grandeur of life.

Touch the ills of the world,
Reduce a little of its sorrow,
Ease a trifle of its burden,
Redeem a sliver of its natural glory.

My life came to its natural end,
A long journey's just culmination.
It crossed your path,
But your way must remain undeflected.
Let my shadow not mar your light,
My history create detours in your plans.
Live for your dreams,
Past will settle by itself.

Do not burden yourself with my absence –
I belong now to the particles of the universe.
Afloat in its timelessness,
Part of its immensity.

I am with you all the time.
You can see me in the gusts of breeze
Greeting the wild flowers,
In blueness of the sky on a clear bright day.

I am in the drops of a rain falling torrentially
After a long sultry day.
In the mysterious calm of a lake;
In the silence on the high mountaintops.

We are bound by eternal love -
The one that does not know the world.
Propelled by its own engine;
It seeks a God unknown.

Elegance At A Rain-ruined Rural Party

She looked out in a serene gaze
At a group of people babbling,
At a well-prepared outdoor rural party,
Ruined by deep drenching, inundating showers.

But was she really looking out?
Her unruffled poise, clean demeanor,
Deceptively casual presence -
All conspired to make her
A well-hidden elegant mystery at the scene.

Many missed her enigmatic allure,
Her outwardly quiet being.
Every human being is partially hidden:
We do not know behind the two still eyes,
Sequestered lie deep desires, fulminating frustrations,
Ruins of the past.

Peering through the lens of my new SLR digital,
I saw a superb shot of hers and jumped at the shutter,
Lest I missed it in a whisper of a moment.
I saw the instant results on the camera screen,
And strode away with a twinkle in my eyes.

Do Not Open The Doors To My Childhood

Why are they urging me to open the doors of my childhood,
Which I had shut stiff a long time ago -
To keep away my still smoldering pains,
To tamp down my recurrently reborn anguished hopes?

I do not want to see my grandfather's cane
Keeping step with me in our jaunts in Shimla bazaars;
Nor his care-worn face gleaming with joy on seeing me;
I do not want to hear my aunt's carefully calibrated voice
Narrating a romantic folk tale in a series of evening sittings;
Neither do I want to feel tormented at the separation with my cousin.

My childhood is a life apart –
A sealed capsule of pristine time,
An island in the stream of my variegated experience.
Its joys are the rapturous blossoms of my existence,
Its wounds the unrelenting spurs of my catharsis.

If I could have done it,
I would have liked to die in my childhood –
To foreclose the ignominy of my later years.
A beautiful blossom of God
Must get defiled through its journey in the world
Before it returns to its sublime eternity.

I want that life to remain sealed
Till I am safely out of this world,
And take it with me to the other world where there is no hurt,
And open its doors there to my joy and happiness.

Father

He remained an aloof tower in my life,
When I was looking for a father.
But the flow of time of has washed my wounds
And now I miss his unalloyed love, his fulsome compassion,
Sharpness of his wit, his unaffected manner.
His presence is imprinted in the recesses of my consciousness,
His incorruptible nobility a light forever shining in my firmament.

You left us suddenly, smiting us to the core;
We needed you in many things that had yet to come.
But you had earned the peace which eluded you in the world.
Now your battles are behind you and you are well anchored
Where angels mingle in serenity and grace.
We wish you could just return for a moment
To see how much better Babu is doing,
How Mummy has lived with a courageous dignity,
And to know the world thinks you put up a splendid fight while here.

The Mood Of An Evening
At Bellmore Island

I am alone at Bellmore Island –
This imperturbable rock in Azelock sea.
The crescendo of the surf and the gusty dance of the winds
Play on the strings of the mind like on a piano.
The mood turns from the rapturous to reflective.

I ask myself what have I done?
What will I do today?
What will I do tomorrow?
And the future looks a blot of ink.
Mornings dawn and suns set,
And time moves in a labored sigh.

She was an angel who did not want to live in a heaven,
But in the clamor and dust of the world -
Among the human beings.
She lived with a passion to give,
To heal others' wounds.
She was not ruffled by the world's slights,
Its materialistic core.

She searched for a God who would make her strong and free,
So she could continue her mission of love and caring.
An ethereal gracefulness enwrapped her;
Her charm was a ribbon of light.
My mother left this world recently;
Leaving behind a footprint of nobility,
A scent of love, a vision of perseverance.

I must return from Bellmore to the world,
To complete my work here on earth.
Then to mingle as a dust with the dust from the stars;
To dance the cosmic dance from which life began.

Dali

A spark has gone but its glow remains

It seems a travesty of reason that Dali has been taken away from us.
Only the other day he was laughing and smiling, thinking and planning.
Where has he gone and why?
Which incomprehensible errand has taken him away
And when will he return?

Dali had the audacity of a smile, glow of a charm,
Unflappable serenity, and impeccable vision,
To cruise through the everyday modern life:
Insensitive and purposeless.

He laughed with bewilderment at the lesser mortals like some of us,
For our unaligned and tenuous connections with life.
He could not think why anyone would not strive to enjoy
And be himself all the time.

He had learnt living at the knees of his life,
His wisdom grew by the simple power of reason.
He had no illusions that life was a gift
Which must be returned to Lord after some time.
What all mattered in life was what we do with this gift.

All the biographies of Dali do not matter.
We may simply say that he came from nowhere
And briefly lit a candle here on earth.
It shown bright and without a flicker.
Many people used it to see things.

His tireless and brilliant scientific work helped and will help
The mankind for generations to come.
His humility was as real as his breath,
His truthfulness was as certain as tomorrow's sunrise.

We do not know how we will go on without him,
How we will be able to harbor joy in our hearts,
How we will be led without a way-shower,
How the family will remain together without the shade of a *chinar* tree?

Thinking Of Surinder

I just returned from Andover, Mass,
Where I had gone to see my cousin, Surinder's, wife, Billy,
And participate in his first death anniversary.
Surinder died suddenly in January of this year, at only 71.

I was first impressed and then amazed by
Billy's stoic and apparently ungrudging acceptance of
Surinder's untimely and sudden death.
Where do some people get such strength from,
In which part of mind reside the buffers
That absorbs the big shocks of life?

After the first day's social meeting,
The next day I sat next to her
In an attempt to assuage her grief,
But soon I realized I was unable to tell her anything comforting,
As she appeared to have accepted the tragedy
And was now moving on in her life.

But her wound had not vanished -
She had dressed it, and left it to heal.
With all my philosophical and poetical trappings
I was rendered into an amiable fool,
As I was unable to say anything good.
The best I could tell Billy was:
Though Surinder prevented many a heart attack in his patients,
But he was unable to do anything about his own.
She seemed to recognize the irony.

The *shraad* that followed appeared
Organized, deftly handled, authentic.
A select group of thirty in attendance showed
Reverence, emotion, and patience for the ceremony.
It was neither too short nor too long.
Dadu and Raju, Surinder's children,
Were the instruments through whom
The *shraadh* connected with the departed one.
It ended with an *arti* which rendered many an eye moist.

On my way back to New York on I- 84
I thought of what goodness, responsibleness, and intelligence
Was lost with Surinder.
Why does God do such rash things?
The absurdity of the question boomeranged on me.
He must have seen a 100,000 patients in his 45 years of medical practice,
He must have cured a vast number of them,
He must have saved thousands from the brink of death.

In this age of emotional coldness
Surinder took extra steps to look up his relatives.
Even though he was kidnapped by terrorists for several months,
He continued to live in Kashmir,
Because he did not know how he could leave his home –
People could not understand this.

A day before he died
He told his family in Goa, where they were vacationing:
He was enjoying the stay very much.
Maybe, that is the way good men die.

shraad: a religious ceremony
arti: prayer

A Light Shines In Andover

He mingles with people with adroit ease,
Making the banter seem spontaneous and smooth.
But little do people know that behind that lie
A lifetime's efforts to acquire wisdom

His developed sense of survival,
His naturalness and modesty are of peasant stock.
He dips into Kashmiri day-to-day wisdom
And folklore to ease the tyranny of modern life.

He has transformed his personal misfortunes
Into absorbents for future pain:
Wounds into wisdom,
Fortitude into faith.

Impossible it is to emulate a master's talents,
Grown as they have through a long immersion
In the search of how to live,
On the merciless saw of life.

He shines through in spite of his efforts
To hide from the insanities of the world.
Brightening the space,
Warming the hearts.

A Marriage Made In Heaven

When gods conceived of human life,
They kept in mind the metaphors of miracle, beauty, and sublimity;
But it seems they forgot that their creation would have to live in the world.

For man the life on earth is the life in the world –
A cocoon he has more or less woven himself –
Strewn with struggle, chance, and unfairness,
Making life a risky adventure,
Dotted by fabulous possibilities,
But anchored in everyday frustrations.

But lurking behind the dark clouds is the marriage of a man and a woman.
It may seem that humankind invented it,
But it is clear that it was created in heavens.
The love between a woman and a man is elemental, stellar –
A force transcending everyday life.
If it were not for this inner fire,
We would not be here.

Debbie and Alan did not meet and fall in love,
But while carrying their already existing invisible love for each other,
They stumbled upon each other, igniting the charge.
Marriages are made in heaven,
Just their framework is provided on the earth.

Reflected in Debbie's and Alan's happiness
We find our own invisible happiness,
We find our own unions with the bliss, howsoever momentary.
It is in God's whole vision of life we find joy,
If we learn to underrate our large egos and little schemes.

Let us wish Debbie and Alan a life of unquestionable love,
Of a creative partnership, and a childlike friendship.
Let this union make them whole and liberated.

For A Life Yet On Fire

Through all these years of life the journey has been good,
Interlaced though it has been with struggle and joy, tears and
laughter.

You look at your journey-partner and think of the journey without
her -
You realize there is color on the horizon and music in the air due to
her.

At this time of celebration let us toast to her glory and our union.
The many tomorrows yet to dawn stand impatiently
To enkindle our energies and paint the skies crimson.

Will They Still Hold Their Hands Together?

_____

Today I stand here and look at the two angelic, wholesome beings;
Poised and puffed up to celebrate the 35th anniversary of their joint enterprise.
Not quite star crossed lovers tied together
By the enduring love born between two persons without reason,
But an unadulterated affection supported by reasoned tolerance,
Accompanied by middle aged tranquility and middle class affability.

We do not know where they met and how they met,
What sly baits Poopan Ji dangled and what sweet non-committals
Nirmal made.
They must have danced around each other for a while,
But in the end Poopan Ji plucked the Kashmiri lotus.
Why would two down to earth and smart persons forge a lifetime alliance
In a risky trouble-prone enterprise called marriage?
We will never know, but we know human life is fraught with equal measures
Of light and darkness, wisdom and stupidity.

While past is a hallowed mystery, present is the only reality we can check.
We know Nirmal and Poopan Ji are two of the sweetest and the
friendliest pals we can find.
Their jug is never empty, their nest is never cold.
They have given friendship another color, they have given community
another name.
While Nirmal is sweet, affectionate, and understanding,
Poopan Ji is always giving, forgiving, and enduring – never asking,
fixing, or blaming.
What Nirmal misses in her double-hugs, Poopan Ji makes up with
his single-malts.
When we enter their home, we know we have stepped into a fairyland.

Their joint venture has produced a magnificent family:
A fabulous pair of girls: poised, gracious, and affectionate.

A scintillatingly lovely grandchild.
The cache is further crowned by a superbly friendly and self-affacing
son-in-law.
Their home is soaked with books and music.
Their life has passed from one golden milestone to another,
Pregnant with grace and courage, purpose and passion.

But there is still work left to be done, there are dreams still to be realized.
But as they pass through the august portals of time,
Through this rough and raucous world,
Will they still feel a tingle in their hearts when they look at each other,
Will they still hold their hands together,
As they walk onward, looking in the same direction?

I Met A Boy In San Francisco

I met a sweet, angelic boy in San Francisco.
His smile was a fountain of spontaneity, a riot of innocence,
He moved in spurts of speed punctuated with sudden stops,
Mischief lurked deep in his face, half-hidden by sly charm,
He seemed always amused and flirtatious,
Babbling away, unmindful of the company around him.

Adults around him saw the magic, conscious they could not
reciprocate in kind,
They simply bathed in his mirth and felt a part of their boyhood revive,
Wondering if growing up has been all that fun.
What are his plans they sometimes wondered,
But the silliness of the question pushed them further into the power
of his spell,
Into the beauty of the moment.

Long after the trip I remembered the delicious delight of his smile,
The rhapsody of his dance, the halo of his curved hair.
Nature at our beginning bestows us beauty and bounce
But the culture and the world trades them for cleverness and material power.
We deny the child in us and create a turmoil in our lives -
Calling it wisdom and hoping to reap a rich harvest from it.

Tricia

Out in Occupational Therapy section of Helen Hays Hospital
Is a light shining and warming the hearts of its patients.
Day in and day out they pass through
This post of basic therapy:
People in pain, slings, and bandages,
On crutches and walkers.
Tricia, Helen, Barbara, Lisa, and Tammy
Greet and treat everyone with serenity and skills.

Tricia and her team not only heal the physical pain
But also balm its mental coefficient.
She has the soft touch - the maternal instinct;
She connects with every patient
In sensitive but solid ways –
Never relaxing on the treatment minutiae.

It is the Tricias of the world that impart value to life.
Seeing her magic I realized that she must have a legion of admirers,
So I stepped back to become an anonymous one.
Tricia go on doing your thing,
You have already painted the sky crimson.

Chasing The Shadows Of Dadu

She came to the party like a princess-
Though without a crown,
To win the hearts of people,
But not to impress their egos.

She moved around with deft grace,
Working her fluid, serene smile,
To connect with people,
Without uncovering her inner-self.

Little does the world know who Dadu is –
As she has carefully covered herself
In layers of sweet amiability and traditional propriety.
She presents herself so perfectly
That it seems she could never do any wrong.

Everyone's life is a presentation to the world
And a presentation to one's God.
The gap between the two is the story of civilization
And for man the still unfinished quest to find the absolute.
We are fortunate to see what we are able to see of her.

Anniversary

The glow of that wedding still lingers on,
Through our triumphs and travails,
Through the ho-hum of everyday life.
We do not know where it comes from
And where it will lead us to
But it has been a beckoning larger than us.

Love is not only looking into each other's eyes
But also looking outward in the same direction.

Our boat is now sailing into the mystic hues of the evening,
And the soft wind is pressing our backs.
Each day has its glimmer, each hour its magic.
Let time dilate and horizon stretch,
And our boat keep on sailing.

It Seems Only Yesterday

It seems only yesterday
When twenty-five years ago today, at bout 11:00 A.M.,
I was ushered into Chief Engineer Joe Zangara's office for a job
interview.
He told me that though I had been in project engineering
The job was in plant engineering.
But he thought that I would be willing to change,
And I was.

Little did I realize that moment
That I would spend the next quarter century
In Lederle's human splendor and its alluring thrall.
It has been more than a job –
It has been a tormenting love relationship –
A magnificent prison sentence without a parole.

But much has changed in Lederle –
Not only just its name.
It has most of the same buildings,
It has some of the same people,
But its spirit does not have the same fire
And its vision does not have the same light.

"Although life must be lived forwards,
But it can only be understood backward."*

Here in 43D/201 was a group of professionals,
Riding the crest of the plant projects and dreams.
From Pharmaceuticals to Research,
From Biologicals to Boiler House.
It was an army with the same uniform,
Bonded with common purpose,

Vibrating on the same wavelength.
It had some of the ablest commanders,
Some of the sharpest soldiers.

An engineer's life here is intertwined with a building's.
(If only buildings could talk,
I would not have had a need to stand here today)
I have worked in almost every building,
Except for the new crop of Research centers.
Some buildings are new and abuzz with smart gizmos,
Though still unreleased from the seize of validation.
Some are old and creaking mad,
Crying for relief of demolition
And deliverance from the ignominy of the new S.O.P.'s.

My story is slowly coming to an end.
When one day I cross the turnstiles the last time,
I would like to turn around and look at Lederle one more time,
And feel the echo of the dreams once I dreamt here,
And sense the serene silence of the buildings holding my work,
And tell myself that I put in the best efforts
Of the best years of my life for this institution,
Then I would know that it was because of your help, your smile, and
your love.

* Soren Kierkegaard

You Came And Lit Up The Evening

You came and lit up the evening
With your gorgeous smile and sweet talk.
Though our roof is small but your heart is large.
We feel every friend is an angel sent our way.
Valentine's Day made us more intimate,
Making us dream that the tender sapling of our love
Grows with time,
Defying the age, skirting the world.

DREAMS OF PAST

Kashmir stands like a Sirius in my firmament.
She has been there in my travails and in my triumphs.
A beautiful maiden, she has been humiliated and marred
By crass human beings who do not know any better.
But she will survive the present withering
And remerge to enchant us gloriously.

Upon Waking Up On My Birthday

I woke up on my birthday to find out when the *guruji* will arrive,
To perform the *pooja* invoking the Gods for my well being.
I waited for the refreshing rub of a new shirt
And the gastronomical seduction of *tahar and charvan.*
The dignifying touch of a *tilak* was missing,
So was the mysterious bond of a *narivan.*
All of these are now interesting relics in the museum of time.
Most of us did not understand then,
And even now, what these sanctified trappings were for.
But we felt we were being connected to something larger than us,
Something within us but beyond the ordinary reach.
Every age has its rituals but birthdays will always have the same message:
To celebrate life and to feel its miracle.

guruji: a priest
pooja: a religious ceremony
tahar and charvan: yellow rice and lamb liver
tilak: an orange colored round mark put on forehead – a religious
symbol
narivan: an orange colored cotton thread tied on wrist – a religious
symbol

A Rendezvous At Habba Kadal

Today, I have laid out my new night suit on the bed,
After carefully ironing it with rice starch.
Also, I have spit-polished my leather shoe to its best wet shine.
Both to be worn late in the afternoon to visit Habba Kadal.
Habba Kadal is the Third Bridge on River Jehlum, in Srinagar.
It is a hub of commercial and social activity.
Filled with grocery vendors, bookshops, and general merchandise shops.
Dr. Chagtoo, a prominent physician, has an office there.

During the day Habba Kadal is a busy town square,
In the early evenings it takes more of a social stage.
Men and women, boys and girls come out here to
Buy things, to converse, and often just to see and be seen.
Young people come to meet their gender opposites for a whiff of a romance,
Superficial in happenings yet real in desire, longing, and hope.

I donned my new night suit with elegant ease
And combed my hair with thick linseed cooking oil,
Creating a lustrous curl-flip rising from the forehead
And dancing down to the mid-ridge.
I marched with controlled excitement for a chance rendezvous with Bimla,
Who schools at the neighboring Vasanta Girls High School,
Where my aunt is the Headmistress.

We met once fleetingly at the school picnic.
She is coy and serene, self-conscious and lovelorn.
She took considerable pains to avoid meeting my continuous gaze on her.
We have never talked and never written to each other
But yet it seems to me an invisible candle has been lit between us.

Today, at four-thirty in the afternoon, I joined a throng of boys
Lined up on one side of the bridge, waiting for the bevy of girls to
Walk on the other side.
Here were two groups, separated by gender,
Who had come to see each other
But pretended to be out on some errand.

The corresponding gazes of each couple locked in
While their legs just carried them on.
Occasionally, the couples looked ahead of themselves
To give a semblance of a regular bridge-crossing.
Not surprisingly the people bumped into each other
When losing track of what was ahead of them.

The bridge romance was as real as a romance could be
Those days in Kashmir.
Love surge of youth had to find an outlet,
Circumventing the terrible taboos of the day.
God created love but man created morality.
Like a summer brook love found grooves and byways
To flow and flood the virgin ground before it.

I searched for Bimla in the crushing stream of girls.
After an infinite waiting I finally found her pair of eyes
And held them into an eternal lock with mine after her response.
Mesmerized thus the two of us walked the entire bridge
Like two zombies lost to this world.
The time thus passed seemed unbounded
And the place we were at did not exist.

The end of the bridge ended our trance
As the paths following it were divergent,
Breaking our gazes, ending the romantic rendezvous.
Afterward, I folded my night suit with diligent dexterousness
For the next gaze-crossing
And wondered how would my unbearable romantic tension end.

Years rolled by and I never met Bimla's eyes again.
I heard she was married and lived happily not far from the bridge.
I also now wonder if she knew my name.
Much as I muse about my run with the flame,
I realize that all I am left with now is a pair of eyes.

Nadir Munjays At Tarakh Halwoy's Shop

Evening has assumed a serene yet exciting mood,
Everything is pregnant with tranquil hopefulness
After day's shattering struggle with survival;
To make money men would stress themselves to death.

I have worn the best night suit I have
And carefully disheveled my hair in a Dilip Kumar coiffure
And slipped on the best *khaddaoon* we had in the house.
Off I go to Tarak Halwoy's sweet shop
To have a good time.

Tarakh Halwoy's sweet shop is near Habba Kadal,
An elite shopping center of Srinagar.
It is a small, dark and dingy place.
Full of cooking utensils,
With little room for the customers to sit and eat.
Tarakh Halwoy himself is rotund and mouth-shut,
Continuously busy cooking sweets in a big *kadai,*
Never bantering with his customers.

Maybe, it was the first take-out in Kashmir.
The shop serves *nadir munjays, dodhu alavs, pakoras, samosas,*
Puris, seemniy, burfi, ladoos, pedas, and other things -
All high delicacy Kashmiri snacks.
Although the place is renowned for its *dodhu alavs*
But *nadir munjays* give me a gastro-delight high.

The scene outside the shop is that of crushing high traffic,
With *tangawallahas* exhorting their emaciated horses with voice and whip,
In the nightmarishly narrow lanes panicky pedestrians scrambling
for their safety
And sometimes colliding with the shop walls.

The scene is soaked with chaos, fear, noise, and excitement.
But those were the sounds and the sights we would want to experience
When visiting Tarakh Halwoy.
In those days of youth, primitiveness, and poverty,
Habba Kadal was our Times Square and Tarakh Halwoy was our
Macdonald's.

Besides the delectations at Tarakh Halwoy's sweet shop
There were delectations at the street in front of it to be had:
Sweet, nimble, love-filled girls walking toward Habba Kadal,
Pretending not to look at Dilip Kumars in the sweat shop
But yet stealing full amorous glances at them,
Contoured with caressing sexy half-smiles.

My visit to Tarakh Halwoy's sweet shop was just an excuse
To have a chance to see Bimla, my dancing heart-throb,
With whom my eyes-only romance
Had been born on the neighboring Habba Kadal bridge,
On which we would walk round and round,
Though in opposite directions of traffic,
With our gazes inter-locked,
Till the street cops and the stray animals
Would look at us with angry suspicion.
Much have I fantasized to share Nadir Munjays
One day with Bimla at the sweet ship.

1. *nadir monjays:* a popular snack
2. Tarakh Halwoy's Shop: a legendary snack shop which
   does not exist anymore
3. Habba Kadal: Second Bridge in Srinagar, which used to
   be its Times Square
4. Dilip Kumar: A legendary film actor of India, renowned
   for his romantic - tragic roles
5. *kadai:* a frying pan

6. *khadaoon*: wooden casual footwear
7. *dodhu alavs, pakoras, samosas,*
   puris, seemniy, burfi, ladoos, pedas, dodhu alavs - popular
   Kashmiri snacks
8. *tangawallahas:* operators of horse-driven carriages

Irrepressible Youth

The Reminiscences Of Amar Singh College Years

Amar Singh College was a big college lying on the south-west of Srinagar,
It is close to Wazir Bagh and Amira Kadal on one end and Jehlum
river flood canal on the other.
Amir Kadal has been the 5th Ave. of Srinagar for generations and will
continue to do so till
Suburban development in Srinagar comes of age.
But the college was considered a notch lower to S.P. College,
The third college of its day in the city.
Amar Singh College was equipped with sprawling grounds
Wrapped in suburban dignity and tranquility.

In fifties when I was a student there the college atmosphere was
highly conservative:
Students were keenly deferential to professors and subservient to
management.
Only in the college tuck-shop and the playgrounds did their
inhibitions melt.
Education was nothing but passing of the exams,
Sports were not a hot attraction then
And girls were more an idea than reality.
But with all its unsophistication it was still fun to be there.

Prof. J,N. Dhar taught physics with a tyrannical control of the classroom.
He threw temper tantrums at will.
He could throw a student out of the classroom for the slippage from
the expected competence or etiquette.
One day he doused a student's head with cold water to make him
behave better;
Another day when a student tried to defend himself against the
professor's accusations in studied English,

He retorted back, "I need an explanation and not literature."
But he knew what he was teaching.

Prof. Nand Lal Darbari was a senior professor of chemistry
But a popular butt of jokes due to his comic appearance and
handling of things.
Once when Principal Mahmood Ahmed had to go on a vacation,
Due to his seniority, Prof. Durbari had to fill in, something he did
not like to do.
Among the very first tasks he had to perform as an Acting Principal
Was to approve a long absence from college application from a
student.
The student arrived with the application in his office and explained
The reason for his request, which was his sister's marriage.
Prof. Durbari was annoyed that he was the one who had to handle
such a request
And told the student, "Did your sister have to get married when I am
an Acting Principle?"

Another time Prof. Durbari arrived in the class after an absence of a
week,
Due to his son's marriage. He sat on the table, with legs dangling, in
his customary manner.
A student shouted at him, asking what was the menu at his son's
marriage reception.
Prof. Darbari went through the list of the items on the menu
And when he finished reading the item *gulabjamun,*
The student slammed back, "Professor, you look like a *gulabjamun.*"
Ever since the nickname *gulabjamun* stuck.

Prof. Yusuf Jandugar taught physics,
He was flamboyant, unsophisticatedly straight, and authoritarian.
He was thin like a reed, tall, and wore a *pagadhi.*
Explaining make and break positions of an electrical device
He would elaborate on the make position of the device at one wall of
the classroom
And then walk to the opposite wall to explain its changing to the
break position.

When he spoke, students listened with complete attention,
Because of the absolute fear they had of him.
He told the class one day that it was alright to swindle, as long as it
was for a large sum of money.
To escape the handcuffs all one had to do is hire an expensive lawyer
from England.

Prof. J.N. Kaul taught English.
Though he was of small-build he was feared.
He used to wear a *Gandhi* cap and limped in one leg.
He gave us a class, on a certain day of the week, at 9:00 A.M. –
It was the first class of the day.
On this particular day he was running late.
All the students were waiting for him on the second floor verandah,
From where there was a clear view of the college bicycle shed,
Where he was going to park his bicycle.
Lo and behold he could be sighted,
Pumping his bicycle pedals furiously.
As he reached the bicycle shed, he quickly alighted from the bicycle,
Swiftly giving it to the shed attendant.
Then he strode, like a tiger, toward the college building.
As the momentum of his stride increased, his sight became very compelling.
Suddenly, I heard some students singing, *badta chal, badta chal,
taroon ke hath pakdta chal......*
This was a refrain from a song of a popular movie, Boot Polish (?),
But as soon as he reached close to the building, the students suddenly
stopped singing.

I have another memory of Prof. J.N.Kaul:
Just before his class it was announced that *Sadarariyast* Karan Singh
was in the process
Of making a surprise visit to the college.
Prof. warned us to be ready for it.
Lo and behold Karan Singh with his entourage entered our class.
He had a big smile on his face and asked the professor about what we
were studying.
Then he asked him who was the shining star of his class.
I felt nervous as I thought I was that person.

To my utter shock the professor just beat about the bush for a few moments
And then announced that there was no shining star in his class.
I could not forgive him for that.
Later, I realized why he did not indicate who the best student was:
It was because of the fear that the best student might have tripped
Karan Singh's questions,
Thereby, blemishing professor's image.

Prof. S.P. Bakhshi would dress immaculately, was well mannered,
and a bachelor.
He taught us chemistry.
He was famous for his statement on why he remained a bachelor:
Jab dood milta hai, gai lane ki kya zaroorat hai.
In English it means: when you are assured of a supply of milk, why
buy a cow.
Prof. Yousuf taught us Charles Dickens' A Tale Of Two Cities.
He would read the text verbatim in his terrible pronunciation:
He pronounced the character Larry as Lorry, the Kashmiri word for
a bus.
After reading every few lines he would warn us: mark humor, mark
drama, mark action,…

Because of the shortage of the girls each girl was special.
God has bestowed on us three at one time.
Indu Raina and Sheela Thussu, Roll Numbers 8 and 303, were my
classmates.
Indu was tall and well-built, while Sheela was slender and of
common proportions.
The former was moderately sociable, while the latter was properly so,
Within the social taboos of the age.
Each day boys would keenly wait for them to arrive in the class
And examine them top to bottom for their attires and moods.
Their smiles were our happinesses; their grey moods were our sorrows.
I nicknamed Sheela, three-not-three, based on her roll number,
Which stuck somewhat.

One day Abdul Ahad, physics demonstrator, called me to his desk,
Just at the beginning of our physics lab.
I was smitten with fear for it was unusual to be called like that.
Abdul Ahad told me that since Sheela Thussu had called sick
I would have to partner with Indu Raina in the experiment as
apparatuses were limited.
I became very nervous with the thought of spending eight hours with a girl
In front of the whole class and the demonstrator.

Within seconds the entire class came to know of my situation;
Boys threw mischievous smiles on me,
For they thought I was in for a great time for the rest of the day.
I was unable to tell them that I was feeling miserable.
Within minutes Indu and I had to stand in front of
The sound velocity measurement by the tuning fork method apparatus.
Indu was taking the lead and I was coyly following her.
Hours passed and we were not getting any results.
It was clear to me, and I guess to her, that our nervousnesses were the
culprits.

Boys inundated me with comments suggesting what a lucky bum I was.
They would not take my assertions of the horrible time I was having.
After the break we resumed our work with lesser nervousness and
obtained some good results.
At the end of the day we were relieved that the torture was over -
The quality of our work was inconsequential.
After some days I felt that in spite of the torture I had experienced
The experience had some sublimity to it -
A romantic languor hung over me for months.
One day the news came that Sheela was ill and would be away from
college for a long time:
She never returned.

The teaching and the whole architecture of preparing students for
higher studies was preposterous.
Classroom lectures were mostly professorial monologues,
Mechanically listened to by the students,
While their hearts and minds were focused on something else.

They knew that all they had to do to pass the exam was
To start opening the books just three months before the exams.
So, why should they put effort to understand and retain what was
being taught now.
Going to college to learn was a big sham: one could have easily stayed
home and learnt more.
The education system was a grand cultural fraud, perpetuated from
generation to generation.
Students just crammed the likely materials questioned in the exams,
To just pass the exams, which was done to get the jobs.
There was no learning and no character building.

Preparing for exams, which would fall during the two month winter
vacation,
Was the highest ordeal of studying.
Students would mug and mug during days and parts of the nights.
Some would get up at 4:00 AM to study.
If overpowered by sleep they would douse their heads under a cold tap.
Understanding the subject material was less important than its
memorizing.
Students would turn into memory machines.
Families would get fully involved with the enterprise.
They would see to it that teas, meals, *kangaris*, etc. were provided.
To get a relief from stress students would refresh themselves by
taking walks.
By the examination time the stress level would have risen very high.
In my neighborhood a boy from a milk-seller family almost suffered a
breakdown:
His appearance and talk changed as the exams approached.

Fridays were half-days due to Muslims' need to go to a mosque.
A few willful students would make rounds of their friend circle
And ask for two *paisas*, which was all they said they needed to
complete the
Seven-and-half *annas* they needed to buy a third-class movie ticket.
Many friends would spare two *paisas,* as this meager amount would let
Their friend see a movie, which was the highest level entertainment
available those days.

Later we would find that the boys did not have any money at all to begin with -
By collecting fifteen two *paisas* they would realize their dream, using mendacious means.

There used to be four girls studying in our rival college, S.P. College.
Boys had nicknamed them: *Badal, Garja, Bijli,*and *Chamki*, keyed to their personalities.
Which in English mean: Cloud, Thunder, Lightning, and Flash.
When I was in the third year *Chamki* moved to our college,
To the great excitement of the boys.
There were two other girls who also moved to our college from somewhere.
They came with their nicknames, Chunnu and Munnu.
I ran for some election in the third-year student body,
For which I had to canvass, which included flesh-pressing.
But my acute shyness prevented me from approaching Chunnu and Munnu.
The loss of two votes in this close election was crucial but my hands were tied.

But toward the end of the canvassing period I was surprised to see the two girls
Approach me, while I was standing in a verandah.
I became nervous, not knowing how to handle myself,
But there was no way I could run away from the impending encounter.
Confrontation finally happened. Chunnu, the petite, slightly chubby girl, my favorite out of the two,
After looking around to make sure no one was watching us, told me that they were going to vote for me.
My excitement at this, mixed with my agitated nervousness, made me just blabber a thank you.
Chunnu emboldened by delivering her message and seeing my nervousness, next asked me
If I needed anything else from her?
Hearing this from her my eyes almost popped out.
I tried to tell Chunnu what I wanted from her but my voice choked and my hands started to tremble.

Looking at my utter misery the girls gave me a tantalizingly
mischievous smile and walked away from me.
I vowed to myself right then that I would never again run for an
election which would have a women electorate;
And I have kept that promise.

F.Sc. practical exam in chemistry was under way:
There was a lot of tension because here was a test
Where mugging could do only so much.
Results had to be produced under the eyes of the examiner
And then one had to go through viva voce with him.
My examiner was Prof. Nasserullah, a very handsome, well-dressed,
and friendly guy.
I did not do badly in the experiment but my shyness was a block I
had to negotiate in the viva.
To my utter shock Prof. Nasserullah's first question to me was: which
was my latest movie?
After easily answering that question, his next question was: who was
my favorite actress?
Emboldened by the answer to the first question I did not mind saying
that it was Madhubala –
An answer I would not have normally given because of my shyness
and inhibitions of the times,
As Madhubhala was a sexy woman.
That was the end of the viva, there were no technical questions.
I was relieved beyond my imagination.
In the evening my uncle by chance met the professor during the
after-office stroll in Amira Kadal,
And asked him how I fared in the exam;
The professor replied that I was very nervous but there was nothing
to be worried about.

Physics practical exam was easier;
Someone in my family, without informing me,
Informed Prof. Triloki Nath Kilam, the examiner,
That I would be taking an exam under him.
Prof. Kilam and we were relatives.
Following day in the lab the tensions were expectedly high.

We waited anxiously as Prof. Kilam walked into the lab:
He was good looking, properly-dressed, and under pressure.
After a few moments he walked across the lab and in his famous
Way of peering over his glasses, whispered in my ears: are you Zind
Lal Kaul's son?
After I nodded he abruptly broke away from me.
Rest of the time in lab was just going though the exam.
But when the results came, I was just awarded about twenty-some
marks out of the forty –
A very mediocre rating; it was clear to me that the professor had not
given me any bonus
Because of our relationship.

The college tuck shop was a buzz of excitement:
Students smoking, drinking tea, talking uninhibitedly about girls
and professors.
There was also talk about movies and politics.
Overcome by the good time they were having,
Many times students would cut their classes.
But the image of the tuck shoppers was bad;
They were considered poor students, drop-outs, irresponsible, and low-level.
And, of course, it was off-limits to girls.

The grounds at the college were open, smooth, serene, and semi-secluded.
Many an hour have I spent looking at them and the associated horizon,
To escape the humbug and the clamor of the world;
They gave me much needed enchanted loneliness.
Friends would sit down under a *chinar* and survey the universe;
We savored moments of delicious gossip and searing conversation.
I spent innumerable hours playing cricket here.
Many classes in summer and early fall would be outdoors, on the grounds.
If there was only one thing I was allowed to remember about the college,
It would be the life on its grounds.

With all the mediocrity of the education provided at the college,
There was still a music ringing in one's soul:
Of the majesty of life, the wonder of nature, the beckoning of the unknown.
Life appeared infinitely rich – an enterprise conceived by the gods;

It seemed to be a calling of very high magnitude,
Everything was touched by grandeur,
Everything was eternal.
With all the life that has flown down since
Nothing has matched the magic of those years.

gulabjamun: a sweet dish
pagadhi: a turban
*badta chal......*keep on moving forward, catching on to the stars....
Sadarariyasat: head of the state
Jab dood milta hai......: when milk is available, why buy a cow
kangris: a portable charcoal burning warmer used in winter
paisas: smallest coin
annas: coin
chinar: a huge maple-like tree

The Agony Of Dal Lake

A stunningly beautiful woman,
Robed in ample, majestic mountains,
Crowned with soaring peaks.
A sublime mother, who for eons has nourished her children,
A cosmic *sanyasin,* who has meditated
For a few million years to be at God's feet –
That is Dal Lake.

I am in a *shikara* surfing the soothing waters of Dal Lake.
After twelve years of exile in U.S. I have come to visit her,
To rejuvenate our relationship, to put back my mind on fire.
But at this moment I feel blown off my feet
In the beautiful agony of meeting my beloved,
After an inhuman lapse of time.

I see from my *shikara* a scintillating, pulsating expanse of water,
Touching the faraway sinewy shimmering shores.
The dance of the wavelets produced by the *shikara*
And caressing cool breeze sets an invisible opera.
This is even before I have set my eyes above the water surface.

What did God have in mind when He created Dal Lake?
Did he want to help Kashmiris with an abundant supply of
Water, cool air, flowers, fish, and vegetables?
Or did he want to create a supremely beautiful place
Which would mesmerize people to believe in a higher meaning of life?

We do not know God's thoughts
But we guess he wanted to do both the things:
He wanted to help his creation in both the physical and spiritual spheres.
But still the overall mystery of Dal Lake is inscrutable:
When and how was it created
And how long will it remain here?

The mountains circumferencing the lake are magnificent.
Their light brown color is sensuously stylish.
They seem to be eternally protecting Dal Lake's privacy,
Cradling a spectrum of gardens in their fluid folds,
A semi-circular ring hugs the lake tightly.
The two islands, Sona Lank and Rupa Lank,
Are two more ornaments embellishing the lake.

Like a celestial visitor, Hari Parbat
Stands in a serene majesty and mystery on the west of the lake -
A part of the whole scene, yet apart from it.
On the south-west, like a sentinel, rises
Shankaracharya mountain and the temple.
Very foreign to the lake but yet blending with its ensemble.

In the distant western background lies the Pir Panchal mountain,
Behind the Zabarwan Mountains skirting the lake,
Stands the awesome Himalayan range in distance,
Making the big picture of Dal Lake huge and complex.
Looking atop Shankaracharaya it is a vast canvass
Brushed with haphazard clusters of dwellings,
Water bodies, and mountains.
There is a mystic quality to the scene:
It seems to have been made by design and with a purpose.
It is so close to us but yet so remote from us.

Dal Lake, including all its tributaries, seen from above
Looks like a baby in a fetal position.
Each of its components: Gagribal, Lokut Dal, Bud Dal, and Nagin
Are special entities but it is the whole, the Dal Lake, which has
The spellbinding charisma, the soul, and the magic.

The Moghul Gardens have gained a legend, an aura, and fame over
Dal Lake.
This is an unfortunate and egregious development -
Staining the truth, squelching the facts.
Moghul Gardens are some 300 years old,
Not upgraded for a long time, crassly ignored in maintenance.
They do not stand much against the world-class gardens.
If it were not for the beautiful mountains behind them
And the stunningly magnificent lake in front of them
They would not be worth writing home about.

What is Srinagar without Dal Lake –
A dirty, disheveled medieval town,
Needing much order and repair.
Any discriminating observer when thinking of Srinagar
Would first think of Dal Lake and its environs.

Shikara-riding the lake opens new scenes of beauty in every direction.
From the shimmer of water and melody of oars drumming it
To the dancing breeze that unrehearsedly greets you,
You find yourself in another universe,
Without an agenda and without a care.
You are transformed from a careful, trained observer
To a consciousness in daze, intoxication, and state of freedom,
In increasing gradations.

You are in a state of a dream,
Drifting from scenic discovery to self-discovery,
Drowned in a half-ecstasy created by the sublime ethereality of the lake,
Wanting to die now and here –
Which would be a crowning achievement
For man's heroic struggle to survive in an ugly world.
We do not know if there is a heaven
But we know that Dal is close to it.

Look at the lake at sunrise and at sunset,
In spring and in summer,
In fall and in winter,

In morning and in evening –
In each setting the lake has a special beauty,
A unique mood.
Like a ravishingly beautiful woman,
It is not one beauty that she possesses
But several, depending upon external circumstances.
While her beauty changes she is still the same:
An ever evolving and yet an ever constant maiden.

As if God had not created an amazing enough phenomenon,
He also created the *rads* – the floating lands in the lake.
They move and can be even stolen.
They are home to vegetables, flowers, and fowl,
Creating a human touch in the tapestry of God.

Have you been on the lake on a summer evening,
When the setting sun paints the horizon golden red?
At that time the dividing road between the Bud Dal and Lokut Dal
Gets transformed into a scintillating silhouette
And the whole scene gets imbued with some divine meaning.

The memories of the old life in Kashmir
Flash bringing in the family trips on the lake in a *doonga*.
For the poverty-drenched life of those days
Such interludes provided the much needed romance of life.

But our ecstasy turns sour,
As Dal Lake is immensely polluted at this time.
Due to its neglect over long haul of time it has
Sediments, poor water quality, weed growth, encroachments.
It has shrunk from 8.5 sq. mi. to 6.9.
A resplendent lake with pristine waters
Has turned into a polluted body of water
And is in a shocking state of disrepair.
The angelically beautiful woman has been
Beaten, harassed, starved, and compromised.

Today Dal Lake moans in pains unnameable,
Cursing its unworthy sons and daughters,
Who besides neglecting her
Have turned the God's Valley into
A political inferno and ignited a religious war.
They have robbed the smiles from the children's faces
And spun them into decades of trauma.
They have divided the two communities
With such brutality that they will remain apart
For generations to come.
The lake mourns the wasting of God's gift of Kashmir
To its crass inhabitants.
In utter sorrow Dal Lake does not know what to do:
Should it disappear or shrink to an insignificant pond?
Only the invisible arrow of time will tell.

sanyasin : a religious devotee seeking God
shikara: a small hand paddled boat
Rad: floating pieces of land
doonga: a boat suitable for living

The Anguish Of Kashmiri Pandits

Walking down the fossilized time,
Revisiting high pinnacles and green lakes
Of spirituality and learning,
Today the old native of Kashmir,
Kicked out of his natural habitat,
Wanders the far corners of the world -
To start a new life, a new community;
To heal his wounds, to follow the old light.

Cut off from its spiritual center,
The community wanders in silent grief,
To find a mooring,
To revive the luminosity that once brightened its universe,
To rekindle the fire that bound it together.
But unable to be reborn,
It gradually drifts into the unnamed universal melting pot,
Turning its hallowed past into history,
Its vision into yet unborn hopes.

The Glory And The Exile

As far as we can look back in the recorded history of Kashmir,
We see a river of Hindus flowing through thousands of years;
Even beyond the recorded history they are thought to have been there.
Five-thousand years of time is some weight for claiming their ancestral
Lineage in their land – a claim that now pierces like a dagger through
their heart.

The name Kashmir is found in unbroken form in ancient Hindu texts:
Nilmatpurana, Ashtadhyayi, Mahabarta, Puranas, and Braht Samhitta.
We know of Gonandiya Dynasty's continuous reign over three-
thousand years.
Legend has it that King Gonanda The First and his son Damodra
Lost their lives fighting in Kureva – Pandava war of Mahabarta.

After thousands of years of Hindu civilization,
Under the new Buddhist convert, King Ashoka,
Buddhism took over Kashmir for the next few hundred years.
It was then the city of Srinagri, later moved and renamed Srinagar,
was founded.
Fourth international Buddhist Council was held in Kundalvan
(Harwan),
In which five-hundred scholars from different countries participated.
Mahayana Buddhism was born there.
Kashmir become the preeminent center of Buddhism,
From where it diffused to Central Asia, Tibet, China, Korea, and Japan.
Lord Buddha is himself supposed to have felt that Kashmir was the
right place for meditation.
In seventh century the renowned Chinese monk Hiuen Tsiang stayed
here for two years.

For two-thousand years Kashmir was an incandescent source of
Sanskrit learning and literature.

It had the intellectual culture to dwell on the deepest human connections
To God, immortality, consciousness, human values, and the mode of living.
It produced some of the most fecund and luminous scholars:
Kalhan, Bilhan, Acharya Bhamba, Udbhata, Acharya Kutanka, Mammata,
Anand Vardhana, Vamana, Rudrata, Kshemendra, Rojanak Shitianth.
A star would light in the firmament whenever Abhinav Gupta
meditated alone on Kahmir Shaivism.
The most tragic point in Kashmir Pandits' history came in 1339,
When Shah Mir founded the Shamiri dynasty paving the way
For seven-hundred years of Muslim rule in Kashmir.
Their torture and humiliation reached its peak under
The fifth Sultan Sikandar, who imposed a tax, *jiziya,*
On people who happened to be Pandits, and banned their use of *tilak.*
Brutally wounded and hounded, so many Pandits left Kashmir that a legend
That only eleven families were left behind was engendered.
As if they had not borne enough suffering they had to endure another
Cycle of torture and humiliations under Pathans and Sikhs.

With India's independence new hopes rose among the Pandits
That their better days were not far off.
In the beginning *Naya Kashmir* sounded a bugle of fairness and freedom,
Only to be dashed by the new wave of discriminations.
New Delhi heavily invested in keeping the Muslims happy,
At the huge deficit of Pandits' economic security and advancement.

Pakistan hungered for Kashmir from the first moment of its creation.
When the beloved did not return its suitor's attentions enough,
It used the ultimate weapon of religious unity and succeeded somewhat.
An insurgency much planned by Zia of Pakistan materialized in 1989,
Killing twenty-thousand Pandits and leaving them no recourse but to
leave Kashmir.
About forty-thousand of them still miserably languish in the refugee
camps of Jammu.
But Pandits' plight has still not moved the GOI –
Engendering a new expression: refugees in their own country.

The supreme irony of Kashmiri Pandits is that today they are asked
who they are?
Being a minority in the present cycle of history,
Politicians wonder if it is absolutely necessary for them to live in Kashmir.
How would the architect of Taj Mahal have felt
If his name were omitted from the history of the monument?
Today's Kashmiri Pandit is a refugee trying desperately to hold on to
his identity;
He is all over the world, trying to continue his ethos.
The community is like scattered leaves in search of the tree they were
shaken off from,
Or the stones of a temple demolished by terrorists
Trying to join with each other to re-form the original shrine.
Pandits are beating their chest about what has happened:
They lived poorly in Kashmir but they were in their home;
They were heavily discriminated against but it did not matter.
But now out of their historical and cultural womb,
Exiled in their own and foreign lands,
They feel the earth is shaking under their feet –
They see the signs of their civilization coming to an end.
Many efforts are being made to preserve their ethos
But the forces of diffusion are strong and they are on the wrong side
of history.
It is still difficult to murmur the words "The Kashmiri Pandit
community is dead,"
But their thoughtful are preparing for that.

When the history of Kashmiri Pandits is written fifty years from now,
It will be noted with irony and pain
That there was a community in the fabled land of Kashmir who
For five-thousand years there reached high levels of philosophy,
religion, and literature;
Who were peace-loving and deeply immersed in religion;
And who were forced to leave their homeland for political reasons.
And their subsequent painful diaspora and diffusion all over the world
Thinned their original personality and culture so much
That their civilization became extinct.

And the history of a thousand-year tormented community came to a tranquil end,
But their story will inspire many a mind and warm many a heart.

But Pandits know that their end in this world, at this time, is not their end in the universe,
Because the universe has no beginning and no end,
What has been created by God once lives forever,
Their spirit is enshrined in eternity.

They will be reborn when the present cycle of Indian history is over,
They will reclaim their paradise and live there as they have always done.

tilak: an orange colored mark put on forehead – a religious symbol
Naya-Kashmir: a political slogan, meaning new Kashmir, coined in 1947 by the first democratic political party in Kashmir

Roots

Touching the ground on which I put the first shaky footsteps,
Seeing the majestic contours of the undulating skyline,
Which my eyes had never tired to range,
Back in Kashmir, I feel the echo of my genesis -
An expatriate's answered prayers.

Buried here lie the pristine years of my childhood,
When wonder turned into thought,
Desires into dreams,
The visions was uncluttered,
And conflict took root.

Does a man owe something to the land of his birth,
Or is it his insecurity that binds him to his roots?
Or is it all an alluring angle of the architecture of emotion,
Or simply an elemental pull to gravitate to one's origin?
If child is the father of man, then what is growing up all about?

Unblemished by the coarseness of life,
Unmarred by the waywardness of the world,
Reposed in the frozen perspective of time,
Still gleaming lie the first experiences of life:

The integrity of self,
The uniqueness of the individual and the brotherhood of mankind,
The uncomplicatedness in human relationships,
The simplicity of understanding,
The unquestioned joy of living,
The clarity of the way ahead,
Just being, not becoming.

We go back to the roots,
To replenish the vision and the spirit we have lost,
To regain our identity and reclaim our history,
To reset the balance between nature and mind,
To feel an element of the universal space-time.

But the chilling vision shattered the trip down the childhood:
Kashmiris living the fossilized glory of their past,
Apathy their unshakable creed,
Cynicism the only energetic hope,
Living between tyranny and anarchy of political pendulum.

Walking down the desolate ruins of Srinagar's streets,
Shapeless stretches of thoughtless construction,
Chaotic services and nightmarish traffic,
Where time has frozen in the inner city,
And darkness envelopes the winter months.

Plundered, ravaged, and defiled through ages,
By its soulless bandit rulers,
Neglected eternally by its crass inhabitants,
To wither slowly in the irreversible arrow of time,
This bounteous gift of nature, Kashmir,
Moans in pains unnameable,
Its soul heaving with curse eternal
For its unworthy sons.

The clandestine evil schemes of 80's
Hatched in some hostile country
Coalesced into one infernal insane fire in '89,
Destroying the finely woven culture of a millennia in the valley,
Disturbing the tranquility of a million years among the mountains.

A friend turned into a murderer,
A neighbor into an arsonist;
A community acquiesced to become an army.
An angelic valley became a death valley –
All in the name of God and religion.

We do not know where to begin anew –
Even, if we should begin at all,
To resume God's work,
To revive the spontaneous sparkling smile
On the faces of a thousand gloomy children,
To let the lotuses grow unperturbed.

We do not know what to do –
Our enemy's brutality has choked our spirit,
Their hatred has tormented our soul.
In one cataclysmic insanity
They have destroyed the Kashmir built by Gods.

But Kashmir always beckons me to homecoming,
A quivering echo of a distant thunder,
A withered glow on the horizon,
Remnant of a fire kindled a long time ago,
It will remain my tombstone.